EMOTIONAL MURDER

Volume 1

Veronica Tucker

Tymm Publishing LLC
Columbia, SC

Emotional Murder: Volume 1

Paperback ISBN: 978-1-7338343-0-8
Ebook ISBN: 978-1-7338343-1-5

Tymm Publishing LLC
701 Gervais St, Suite 150-185
Columbia, SC 29201

Editor: Glenda Wright
Proofreader: Kiera J. Northington
Cover Design: Tywebbin Creations

Dedication

I dedicate this book to the late Mr. Edward Hoard and Florence Taylor Hoard, my beloved parents. God allowed them to come together to bring me here to earth to do His will. I would also like to dedicate this book to the citizens of the Kingdom of God and everyone all over the world.

Acknowledgements

I honor the King of kings, Alpha and Omega. I would like to thank the King of glory for guiding me through the process of putting this book together. I realize how much this gift of writing is a part of my mission of reconciliation. I died to religion and awoke to my Kingdom credentials as a Kingdom citizen, ambassador, and daughter of the King. Faith in the Kingdom has made me free. It has given me the power to believe in my passion and pursue my dreams. Writing a book is harder than I thought and more rewarding than I could have ever imagined. None of this would have been possible without the faith I have in You, the Almighty God.

To my firstborn child, God's son, Tylon Tucker, I thank you for challenging me. Your insight and thought process from the views and behavior of a millennial has opened me up in many things. I admire the level of knowledge and understanding you possess as a young person.

To my second-born child, God's daughter, Tyecola Tucker. For a long while, I thought we were totally opposite; however, in the last few years, I realize the benefits of our relationship. We challenge each other, learn from each other, and it's all balancing out as we both mature in our role of mother and daughter.

To my third-born child, God's son, Dayronn Tucker. I always say you are the best part of all of us, your dad and me, grandparents, and your older siblings. I admire your faith, tenacity, and persistence in following your dreams.

To my grandchild, God's son, Joshua Messiah. The best grandchild ever, anointed and chosen, He made me GRAND.

I thank God for the several special colleagues and friends who have connected with me through social work.

To my spiritual colleagues, family, and friends, I want to thank each of you for supporting me wholeheartedly in my God-given projects. I love you all beyond measure.

Kingdom blessings to the royal citizens of the Kingdom of God.

Table of Contents

Introduction

Trauma is defined as having an extreme disturbing event or experience that impacts a person psychologically, spiritually, and emotionally. Trauma can present itself in several ways: domestic violence between a spouse or romantic partner; grief, sexual abuse, neglect, serious accident, extreme illness, victim or witness of a violent crime, or natural disaster. Trauma has the ability to leave its victims in shock, denial, disbelief, confusion and difficulty concentrating, anxiety, fear, depression, and post-traumatic syndrome. It may cause guilt, shame, and self-blame, withdrawing from others, disconnect from society, or even worse, death.

Emotional Murder is the story of a young, southern girl named Rhonda Jones. It describes the various traumatic events that she encountered and illustrates how these experiences shaped her life and impacted the lives of those around her.

Rhonda's story teaches us why developing an awareness and understanding of your emotions is very important. With practice, your ability to recognize, tolerate, and regulate your emotions will improve. Increased emotional self-awareness is key to achieving success. How will success be achieved? Through Rhonda's story, we will become aware that showing emotions does not represent a sign of weakness. It is a healthy social skill to have as you are able to manipulate even your toughest enemies and competitors to believe you are strong even when you feel weak, victorious even when you feel like a victim, and be able to empower others even when you feel powerless.

Rhonda's story represents the many teens and young adults all over the world who may have experienced an array of traumatic events and are coasting through life emotionless. Like Rhonda, many of us are never educated about feelings and how to properly express them. Instead we learn socially acceptable ways to deal with our feelings by imitating the people around us.

As a result of being unable to properly express her feelings and dealing with her feelings in inappropriate ways, Rhonda has died an emotional death.

The information illustrated through Rhonda's story was inspired by true events. Names and identifying details have been changed and or dramatized to protect the privacy of individuals.

Chapter 1

RHONDA JONES

I was born May 3, 1973. My parents suffered two tragic losses before successfully becoming pregnant with me. I can't imagine how it must have felt for Mama to silently grieve the death of each child and carry on life with a business as usual attitude. She was expected to continue performing her wifely and parental duties.

Because of the unique circumstances from which I was formed, I've always taken the bull by the horns. I dealt with life in a brave and decisively direct manner with no regards to dangerous or unpleasant situations. When I wanted something done, I got it done. Whatever I wanted in life, I got it. There was nothing too big or small, wide or large that I feel I can't acquire or accomplish. The number three had always played a significant role in my life. Number three was said to be the meaning of natural affirmation, self-reliance, and confidence and the faith you need in yourself to walk in your purpose and achieve your desires.

On the downside of this, I struggled with finding the right people. Perhaps that was my problem in life. I couldn't seem to find anybody or establish the proper relationships and friendships that could keep up with the speed that I like to move in. I had plenty of so-called friends, and I've never met a stranger. I did have a way with people to get what I wanted, when I wanted it. Did that make me a manipulator? Maybe. Maybe not. At times, I couldn't be satisfied in life because I wasn't satisfied with the direction I'd gone or the results I manifested. Sometimes, I wanted to take off this superwoman cape and avoid the difficulties of disappointments that kept me from moving on like everyone else. At times, when dealing with certain issues, I almost wished I were invincible. But suddenly, depending on the day of the week or the people in my life, it seemed like a burst of confidence came over me, and I was okay.

I guess you could say I am a professional survivor with a side of generational affliction. Sometimes I felt blessed, but oftentimes, I felt cursed. My life experiences could best be described as a walking zombie, coasting through life, no longer experiencing happiness or pleasure from my existence. This was the place where feelings of anger, rage, fear, happiness, empathy, and positivity no longer exist in your prefrontal cortex.

How could this be? Growing up, it appeared that I had the perfect life. My parents loved me and treated me like a southern princess. Anything I wanted, my father made sure I got it. My mother sheltered me. My father protected me. If I wanted my favorite ice cream before dinner, my daddy made sure it happened. If I wanted a new dress, my mother would buy it. In fact, I loved getting dressed and going to church. It was a tradition our family loved and participated in, and I did not mind. I liked going to church to show off my new dresses and bows. I enjoyed the singing and sometimes the preaching. It was good entertainment. The fact is, I grew up in a home where seeds of spirituality were dropped in my spirit, the word of God was read on daily basis, but I would get confused because the principles of the Kingdom of God were not fully explained. I had conflicting information, but that did not keep me from believing in God and praying.

I remember it like it was yesterday. I sat on the porch, swinging my legs back and forth, and the clouds appeared to be a little dark. I prayed to God that it would not rain even though I loved the rain because it reminded me that God was showering His blessing on my life. I hated the hot weather. The South was known for its hot weather. For that reason, winter and spring were my favorite seasons. The sun filtered through the clouds, signaling the end of the rain. I felt a cool breeze across my face, letting me know there was a blessing just for me. I felt joy bubbling up inside of me. Suddenly, the sun appeared, and it beamed down on the back of my neck. It was blazing hot. I ignored the heat and dared not complain because I was more focused on the day being Sunday, one of my favorite days of the week.

When God answered my prayer and didn't allow it to rain that day, it just confirmed how much of a southern princess I really was. Even God favored me and always gave me what I wanted.

Mama always dressed me up in bright colors. I don't remember having a favorite color. I always believed there was a connection between colors and our feelings. Mama was a melancholic type of person; she relied on facts instead of speculations. She could be skeptical and suspicious, and she was rough, but tender when it was needed. I randomly caught this glare of sadness in her eyes. I guessed that was why she liked to keep me dressed in bright colors, so when she saw me, I would brighten her day. Because I knew dressing up made her happy, it made me happy. After she got me dressed, I would stand up, close my eyes and swirl around a few times, opening my eyes a few times to make sure I didn't fall and get dirty from being dizzy. Mama did not like it when I got dirty. "Only tomboys get dirty!" she said. I did not know what a tomboy was, but obviously, it was someone who gets dirty.

Mama coordinated my outfits. I loved the sienna silk and crepe dresses, the kind that Shirley Temple wore in her movies. Yellow and white were Mama's favorite colors. Yellow represented happiness and courage, while white represented peace and purity. She even dressed me in little yellow and white bloomers with the yellow and white bows to coordinate. I felt fresh, happy, and beautiful. I knew it was a beautiful day God had created, and I felt energized and optimistic.

Mama yelled, "Rhonda, come take off your dress and shoes and put on a pair of short pants and tennis shoes."

I asked, "Mama, can I put on another dress that's not my Sunday dress with my tennis shoes?"

She answered, "I guess so."

I ran inside to change, and I snuck out my little radio. One of my favorite things to do was to listen to music. The whole family loved music; it was one of the highlights of Sunday dinners. I took an interest in musical expression because music had a way of verbalizing emotions I didn't know how to communicate. The rhythm, paired with harmony and dynamics, made me feel alive on the inside.

Mama said, "I don't want you listening to grown people's music."

I'm not sure where I first heard Stephanie Mills, but I loved when the song, "Home," played on the radio. I loved her voice because it was so soothing, and I could tell she was singing from her soul. Mama didn't allow anything but gospel music in the house on Sundays. But,

I always got my way, even if it meant risking getting in trouble by disobeying her authority. Music became my passion. It had a way of healing my soul and altering my mood. I believed in the arts and entertainment through paintings, drawing, writing, and taking photos. It was an outlet to express how you feel without talking. I enjoyed talking, but it was no secret that I struggled with finding the right words to express what I was feeling.

I lay back on the porch swing and played the radio while waiting for everyone to arrive for Sunday dinner. Mama normally was right there on the porch, watching me like a hawk. She was always very protective of me, especially when I started going through puberty. She refused to let me out of her sight. Anytime I could steal a moment away from her and catch up with my cousins, I took full advantage of it.

Mama was meticulous about her food; she was proud to cook for her family. The only time anyone was allowed in the kitchen was if she invited them to taste test. Everyone knew not to go in her kitchen while she was cooking. She was very passionate about cooking, and her kitchen was her sweet, safe haven. It was one of the most joyous activities in her life. She grew her own vegetables, and there was always fresh fruit around for a snack. Mama was focused and didn't have time to see what I was up to. Sometimes, she would call my name while in the kitchen to make sure I was still in the front yard. She wanted me to be the taste tester at times, but I avoided it. I told her I was not hungry, or I had a tummy ache. I preferred to listen to my music and wait on the family to arrive.

This particular Sunday, the entire family was coming over for Sunday dinner. I had written this song and wanted to perform it with my cousins for the family. Uncle Jack and Auntie Ashley, some childhood friends of my Daddy's from Atlanta, Georgia, were in town and were coming over for dinner. I had not seen them in forever. A few of my dad's co-workers were coming over, as well as a host of cousins, aunties, and uncles. This was my time to shine! I liked when our family hosted family dinners. Because of my parents' role in the community, the doors to our home were always open. Our home was the place you could come to find love, acceptance, understanding, and refuge.

I always felt safe and secure at our family home, surrounded by a community of people who respected my parents and their children. We considered everyone as family, and it did not matter if they were blood-related or not. Everyone in our family loved to entertain or to be entertained. Mama was still busy in the kitchen, so she didn't notice what music was playing. The whole family was enjoying the music, singing and dancing. The adults often formed a "Soul Train line," and the children and teens came down the aisle, showing their best dance moves. The best dancer took home five dollars. When I was younger, I got upset because my older cousins always won the dance contest. Uncle Larry still gave me a dollar because he felt pity for me. He used to say, "Be original and dance by yourself next time."

Daddy would always get on him and say, "Leave my girl alone, Larry!" We all knew Larry meant no harm, but that is how much Daddy protected me. He would never let anybody say or do any wrong towards me.

For our family dinner dance off this time, as each person danced down the "Soul Train line," I would perform my song with the help of my favorite cousins, Erica and Jan. Erica and Jan were my blood cousins. Jan and Erica agreed to be my backup singers and dancers, while Case was our hype man. Jan and Erica were the only girls in the family around my age, so we were pretty close. During our performance, we put on a show!

The whole family talked about how well we did! We had the entire house jamming to our song.

When the crowd started to separate, Mama went off to the kitchen and began cleaning up. I went in to help her tidy up and possibly get her feedback on my performance. Before I could get anything out, Mama asked me, "How do you feel about Jan, Erica, and Case living with us full-time?"

I thought, *Wonderful*! We can go to school together, and I can have all my favorite people together under the same roof! Their dad was in the military, and they traveled a lot. Uncle James felt it was best to have the children in a more stable environment so they could make childhood friends and improve their social skills.

Uncle James was very mean. Rumor had it that the military made him crazy. He always had nightmares and slept with his gun under his pillow. Nobody knew what was happening with his wife. It's something the family didn't speak on. Jan and Erica were very smart and mature for their age. They learned how to read at an early age and were very polite and pleasant in their speech. The two of them were eighteen months apart in age, so they acted more like twins. Erica, the oldest, was very clever with getting whatever she wanted out of her father. Jan was the "go along to get along" type. She avoided conflict at times, especially with Erica. Erica was not someone you wanted on your bad side. They say she had a temper like her daddy. Case was easy going, barely made a sound. If it was not for the food disappearing in the house, you would not even know he was there! The children loved their father, but they did not want to live with him because of his nightmares. It was a win-win for everyone when we discovered they would be moving in with us. I only had good memories of Uncle James. When we were little, he used to give us piggyback rides, buy us butter pecan ice cream, and drive us around in his shiny, blue convertible.

As the weeks and months went by, I was excited to have Erica and Jan around. We used to dance our hearts out! Our favorite song to dance to was "Ain't No Stopping Us Now," by McFadden and Whitehead. This song brought back many happy memories, but on this day, it did not. Jan stopped in mid-dance and burst into tears. I asked Jan what was wrong. Erica was a very strong girl, and she rarely cried.

Erica responded, "She's whining because she's going to miss Daddy. He is going away to Germany for a very long time. I miss hanging out with my mom, but you don't see me crying about it." Erica and Jan had not seen their mother in almost a year. Their mom hardly ever came around the family. When she made an appearance, it was short and sweet.

Jan was angry and yelled, "Shut up, Erica! You always telling our business! Ugh!" Jan said she was going to move to Germany with Uncle James. "Oh, you will see, Erica; you will see!" and she ran off into the house and started packing her things.

Erica followed her, shouting, "Stop being a baby, Jan! Nobody wants to hear Mommy and Daddy fight all the time! Let him go to Germany or whatever, so we all can have peace!" By this time, Mama heard the commotion and asked what was going on. All of us stood there in silence, looking at Jan.

Mama believed in the power of prayer. Anytime a conflict arose, she believed we should pray. She pointed to the floor and on our knees we went. She said, "Call on God and demand the angels in heaven to terminate every evil assignment of the enemy."

She sensed the tension in the room between Erica and Jan. She shouted out with authority, "This house belongs to God, and no demon in hell will enter into it!" Jan and Erica apologized to each other, and Jan removed her clothes from her bag.

Chapter 2

MR. LAWRENCE
Exhibit A

What made the relationship between Jan, Erica, and me so special was that we all loved to sing and perform. The porch was our stage, and anyone in passing was our audience. One of our favorite shows to watch was *Showtime at the Apollo*. I pretended to be Ki Ki Shepard and have whoever in the audience judge Jan and Erica on their performances. Sometimes, Case, Mama, the kids in the neighborhood, or Mr. Lawrence were the judges. Of all the people who used to watch our porch performances, there was something strange about Mr. Lawrence.

Mr. Lawrence lived three doors down from us. He had to pass our house to get to the corner store or back down to the road to get back to his house. Mama used to work with his stepmom back in the day. Mr. Lawrence sometimes talked to himself while he was walking. He was often in full conversation mode, even though there was nobody around him. If we were performing, he always stopped by to enjoy the show and clap at the end. Daddy used to say Mr. Lawrence was crazy, just like his mammy. He was in his early twenties, but he was small in frame. He could pass for around fifteen or sixteen years old.

Mr. Lawrence made Jan very uncomfortable to perform. "That guy gives me the creeps," Jan said.

Erica thought Jan was being a brat and responded. "How are we going to get better with our performance if we don't practice and entertain the crowds?"

Jan said, "Y'all can do whatever y'all want, but I'm not performing for no weirdos." Because Jan and Erica were older than me, I always stayed out of their disagreements and sided with Erica, since she was the boss. Because Erica did not have anyone to compete with, she gave in and decided to ride bikes with Jan.

Riding bikes was fun! We pretended we were riding to New York to perform at the Apollo and go shopping with the rich folks. One day we rode for so long and so far, we ended up at an abandoned barn in the middle of a field. Mama and Daddy owned all the land that surrounded our home, so it was no big deal to go exploring. Mama watched us like a hawk anytime we were outside playing, but this time, Auntie Pam came over, and they got carried away sipping tea and gossiping. We used that opportunity to explore a new area. We had lived in this neighborhood since before I was born, but I never left the front porch.

When we arrived at the abandoned barn, we thought it would be fun to play house there. Inside, there were dusty pots and pans on a rustic firewood stove. About one or two windows had cracked glass, but allowed the sun to shine through. There was old furniture, clothes, and storage containers present as if someone used to live there. Before long, this was our new clubhouse. We met there several times a week to play and pretend it was a house. One day, Erica sorted through the things in the old storage bins. Jan and I removed debris and dusted so we could turn our playhouse into a play home. We all talked and sang during our cleaning, and I noticed Erica became extremely quiet. As the sun began to set, it was time to go back home. Erica was distant the rest of the afternoon. She did not speak much over dinner, and she tossed and turned all night in the bed.

Over the next few days, this behavior continued. Jan and I grew very concerned because we thought she was sick or getting ready to start her menstrual cycle.

When we arrived at the playhouse, I asked, "Erica, did we do something wrong? You have not said much to us in a few days. Are you sick?"

Erica said, "No. Just have a lot on my mind."

What could possibly be on Erica's mind? She was not dating anyone at school, and we all kept each other secrets. Then, finally, Erica just let it rip. "Jan, I am not trying to be mean, but I want you to see Daddy for who he really is. He is not the man we thought he was."

"What do you mean, Erica? We have not seen Daddy in months? He's in Germany, remember?" We thought Erica was losing it! Then Erica went to the storage bins she was sorting through and showed us several pictures of Uncle James and some children and a whole family we knew nothing about.

"Erica, what is this?" I asked.

"Look Jan! Look! This whole time, Daddy has been lying to us! Look at these children; they look just like us, Jan!" That day, we discovered Uncle James had twin girls and a girlfriend. Maybe that's why their mommy never came around the family. Maybe that's why they argued all the time. Maybe that's why he was moving to Germany.

Jan replied, "Erica, you are always so negative! You would do anything not to see Mommy and Daddy get together again!" By this time, Erica and Jan were face-to-face, yelling and screaming at each other. I did the best I could to break up their arguing, but it was as if I was not in the room with them. The whole time Jan and Erica argued, I kept hearing a sound.

"Hey guys, do you hear that?" Finally, they stopped arguing long enough to hear the noise.

"Yeah, I hear something," Jan said.

"I hear it too!" replied Erica.

"What is that?" We all became very spooked and began cautiously walking around the playhouse looking to identify where this noise was coming from. Out of nowhere, Mr. Lawrence appeared. "Mr. Lawrence!" we all shouted in fear. "What are you doing here?"

Mr. Lawrence replied, "What are you girls doing here? It's not safe out here."

Erica replied, "What does it look like we're doing? We are having girl time, no boys allowed."

Mr. Lawrence replied back, "You have a sassy mouth, girl! And you have no business being out here this far away from home. Go on back home before you girls get in trouble."

Jan said, "You are not our daddy. Who do you think you are? We are having fun minding our business." Mr. Lawrence exited the playhouse with a mysterious glare on his face.

To change the tension between Erica and Jan, I suggested we keep this secret just between us until we have more proof that Uncle James had more children and another woman. Jan and Erica agreed to keep this between us and not disturb the rest of the family with this information. On our way back home, we stopped by the corner store for some snacks. Mr. Lawrence was also at the corner store, sitting on a bench, having a conversation with himself.

When we left the corner store, I suggested we play red light-green light. Mr. Lawrence overheard our conversation and thought red light-green light was so boring.

"You girls are too big to be playing red light-green light. Why don't y'all play something else?"

I replied, "What do you have in mind, Mr. Lawrence?"

"Hide and seek. That's 'bout you girls' speed since y'all like hiding away in barns and whatnot."

Erica replied, "Sure, why not?" Erica got bored easily and was always looking for new adventures. I was really good at red light-green light and would win every time. I never played hide and seek before.

Mr. Lawrence explained how the game should be played. One person counts while the other players go hide. Whoever was found first would have to be the counter and the seeker for the next round. I was a very fast runner when playing red light-green light, so I went first during round-one of hide and seek. We had ten minutes to find all the players. Whoever was not found within those ten minutes won the game. Mr. Lawrence had a watch on, so he agreed to keep time.

The last person to seek was Erica. As Jan and I were hiding, Mr. Lawrence said it was a good idea to hide in an old, abandoned car in his yard.

"Rhonda, come over here. They are never going to find you in here!" Because Mr. Lawrence was the time keeper and had observed where the other girls had hidden before, I trusted his judgement. I heard Erica counting to ten. "One... two... three... four... five... six... seven... eight... nine... ten. Ready or not, here I come!" As Erica ran around our playhouse and Mr. Lawrence's house, looking for me and Jan, Mr. Lawrence told me to keep my mouth shut, or I would lose the game. Time was up, and Jan was found. I heard them both calling out for me, "Rhonda, where are you? Come out, Rhonda!" Mr. Lawrence said time was not up yet, and I should remain quiet for a little while longer so I could officially win the game.

"Okay," I decided. I hated losing at anything.

When the time was up, Mr. Lawrence asked me what I wanted for winning the game.

"Some candy would be fine," I replied.

As I was gathering myself to exit the car, Mr. Lawrence said, "I have something better than candy." He grabbed me by the arm, pinned me down, and he forced his hand inside of me. "Mr. Lawrence, what are you doing?" I cried out.

"Giving you your surprise, baby girl. Now, you promise not to tell anyone about this, right? Because if you tell, you will not be able to come outside and play anymore."

I was confused by what had just happened. But, I knew I could not tell anyone, because I did not want to be the reason Jan and Erica would no longer be able to play outside.

By this time, Erica and Jan were growing concerned about my whereabouts, and they had gone inside to tell Mama Jones. I heard Mama yelling for me three houses down. "Rhonda! Rhon-da! Don't make me come looking for you, gal!"

I took off running for the house. "Here I am, Mama!"

Mama asked, "Where were you?"

I replied, "I was in the back yard! We were playing hide and seek, and I was waiting for them to come find me!" Mama gave me a look like she knew something was not right.

Later that night, I lay awake in bed. I did not know how to explain the emotions that came over me. It was a mixture of disgust, embarrassment, confusion, enjoyment, and guilt. I went back and forth in my mind, not sure who to blame for the trauma I was experiencing. Maybe I was at fault. I allowed myself to get too comfortable with Mr. Lawrence, knowing he was crazy. Maybe it was Erica's fault. She always got bored easily and was looking for a new activity to play. Or, maybe it was Mama's fault for allowing us to slip away from the porch. If Mama ever learned of the events that took place today, I knew it would break her heart. I had to protect Mama.

Emotional Murder

Chapter 3

MAMA JONES

Mama Jones was born in the late 1920s. She was the youngest of three children. She was a one-year-old when her mother, Mable, passed away. Mable went into labor at home and was preparing to give birth to another child. Suddenly, something inside her ruptured, causing her to lose a lot of blood. Before the elders and midwives could arrive to help her, it was too late. Mable and the baby both died, leaving Mama, her brother, and sister motherless. After Mable's death, Mama and her siblings were raised by her father's mother, Sallie Mae. Mama's dad could not bear Mable's loss and did not know how to raise children.

Great-Grandma Sallie kept Mama and her siblings, along with three other cousins. So, you can imagine her house was very crowded, so crowded that Mama had to sleep on the floor and share bath water with the other children. However, she managed to keep to herself. Great-Grandma Sallie stayed in church, so it's no secret that Mama loved the Lord too. She loved praying, worshipping, and reading her Bible.

When Mama was of age to work, Sallie took her along with her to the fields to pick cotton. She also helped clean the house, cook dinner, and bake cakes.

She did whatever she could to lessen the burden her grandma carried. Years passed by and she hadn't seen her father again, but heard through family gossip that he quickly remarried after Mable's death. When Mama shared this story with me, I was angry. How could a parent abandon his children like that? Mama, being the rational thinker that she is, always said, "I was not abandoned. I was raised by someone who loved me. I had a roof over my head, food to eat, and that's all that mattered." That's what I loved about Mama. She was always able to see the glass as half full. I never heard her speak bad about her father or about Great-Grandma Sallie.

Mama's dad, Reid, came back into her life when she was in the fifth grade. I guess he felt like being a dad again since his new wife, Lillian, had two children he'd fathered and needed help around the house. Reid came to Sallie's house one day and said it was time for him to take the children home. And just like that, she packed up what little belongings she had and went back home to live with her dad and stepmom.

When she went to live with Reid and Lillian, she had to eventually quit school and get a job to help out with the household expenses. Lillian preferred her children not to work because she wanted them to be productive in school. But, Mama was very smart and wise beyond her years for someone who only completed fifth grade.

This behavior did not last long because she grew tired of working to support Reid and Lillian's household. When she turned eighteen, she quickly married her first husband and considered herself free from Reid and Lillian's plantation.

I sensed Mama was not happy or suffered from what we now know as depression while she was living with Reid and Lillian. Here was this man who was her father, but who had never fathered her since she was born. Instead, he only came back for her so she could serve as a maid for his new family. In my dreams, I could see things like on a movie screen. I saw Mama as a young child, perhaps five years old, expectant, dressed up for her big day, waiting with such anticipation but constantly and consistently disappointed because her dad had not come for her yet.

Mama loved her grandmother, but she missed her mommy. I felt in my dream that she was alone and scared. She was kneeling, praying to the Lord to heal the wound of abandonment. This could explain the sadness in her eyes. She was indeed a praying woman. Each night for as long as I could remember, she read the Bible and prayed afterwards. Mama never prayed out loud; she sat instead of kneeling, and I would hear, "Yes, Lord," like she was in conversation with God. I was sure whatever she and God talked about touched the lives of those around her.

She called on the name of Jesus very often. She sat on the side of the bed and said, "Lord, help me to hold out until my change comes." I imagine this was when she may have been in distress. Mama had me pray out loud. She started me off, but I had to finish. She said, "Our Father, who art in heaven."

Then I finished with, "Hallowed be thy name. Thy kingdom come. Thy will be done, as in heaven, so in earth. Give us day by day our daily bread. And forgive us our sins for we also forgive everyone who is indebted to us. And lead us not into temptation but deliver us from evil. God bless Mommy and Daddy." Then, I would name every relative and friend I could think of.

After a while, Mama would say, "God bless everybody in the whole world. Good night!"

Undoubtedly and unintentionally, we were taught by our parents how to approach our lives and relationships. According to Mama Jones, men took care of women by bringing home their paycheck. She left her first husband after he stopped working and was no longer providing for her and their three children. She said, "If a man cannot take care of his wife and children, he isn't a man. Love doesn't pay no bills."

Mama Jones loved the Lord, and we were in church at least three days a week. I always felt like I never knew her the way her older children did. I knew the Mama Jones who served on the missionary board and the usher board at Beloved Missionary Baptist Church. I knew the one who did not drink, and read her Bible every night. She was Mama, who was there when I came home from school and always had a full-course meal spread out on the table. Going to church was pretty much our bonding time. During the time of getting ready for church, I noticed she would be more talkative and would say things like, "We don't meet people by accident. They are meant to cross our path for a reason. It may be to build us up or to break us down. They will come and go but don't focus on how long someone stays. What we learn from everyone who passes through our lives is most important."

She also said, "Be prepared. Some lessons are expensive, but all are priceless. Every struggle is a test of your faith." She said things without much explanation. As I got older, I was able to understand what they all meant.

Mama said, "Girls are to be seen, not heard." Whenever I was expressing how I feel or giving an opinion, she always viewed it as talking back or being disrespectful. She had high expectations of me.

Mama Jones called me her "change of life baby," because her menstrual cycle had begun to change, and the doctor told her that her hormones were getting ready for the "change of life." Daddy Jones and Mama had already conceived two babies, both boys. One survived about six months; the other survived only three weeks. Both babies got very sick, but no one could ever tell Mama what was actually wrong with them. Some years passed, and she missed a period. She thought, *Oh, change of life*! When she missed two periods and had other symptoms, she went back to the doctor's office. The doctor prescribed some medications to help with the bad stomach cramps. A nurse at the doctor's office decided to get her a pregnancy test. Her life was changing all right, nine whole months of changing. It seemed that the hormonal shift was just right for her to be able to get pregnant, proving that I was born with a purpose from the start. I was birthed with love, joy, and peace. I was to complete some things in my generation.

Babies born after a miscarriage are considered to be rainbow babies, so it was no coincidence that I was born on the third day of the month, while a rainbow was present. Mama believed that the rainbow was a sign of God's promises and new life. Both of my parents believed I was a miracle baby who made their lives complete.

Emotional Murder

Chapter 4

DADDY JONES

Born and raised in Atlanta, Georgia, David Jones, better known as my daddy, was the oldest of several children. I had so many aunties and uncles on my father's side of the family that I couldn't count or keep track of them all. Daddy was what they call eye-candy. He stood six feet four inches, was bow-legged, had smooth black skin, and a crisp white smile. Before he met Mama, he had a thing with the ladies. He could pull any woman he wanted. The ladies at the church flocked to him like bees and honey.

Daddy appeared to be an open book, but there was always a mysterious side to him. We never talked much about his home in Atlanta or about any of his siblings, cousins, aunties, or uncles. Both of his parents died when he was younger. He relocated from his hometown and moved to South Carolina because he needed a fresh start. He had no blood relatives there, so I'm not sure why he chose to relocate there. He never went to visit anyone in Atlanta that we knew of.

Daddy met a woman named Annie shortly after moving to South Carolina. The relationship escalated quickly, and three children were born from it. Unbeknownst to Daddy, the woman was married when she had those children with him.

Annie's husband was in jail for drug trafficking, and she considered their relationship over. Her husband, Mike, did not get the memo. He served seven years of a twenty-five-year sentence and was released from jail. Mike heard through his friends in jail that Annie had given birth to three children by some city slicker from Atlanta. Mike felt violated and like that was a personal attack from my daddy. The day Mike was released from prison; the first thing he did was visit the pawn shop and purchased a .45 caliber pistol, with matching bullets. Afterwards, Mike went to Annie's house in a drunken rage. The neighbors heard the commotion and started gathering outside to see what was happening.

Bam! *Bam*! *Bam*! "Open the door, Annie! Open this door right d@mn now!"

Mike was furious! Daddy and Annie were in the house with the children eating dinner. Being the protector he is; Daddy went outside to confront Mike, man-to-man. Mike didn't have anything to talk about. Before Daddy could open the door, he fired several rounds into the house. The children were screaming and crying; Annie was a hysterical mess, and there was blood everywhere.

"Call an ambulance! Somebody's been shot!" one of the neighbors shouted. My daddy lay in a pool of blood. Mike fled the scene. He knew the damage he had caused and feared going back to jail.

Each time Daddy shared this story with me, I became more emotional than the last time he shared it. If he would have died, there would be no Mama and Daddy. I would have never been born, and this beautiful life they created for me would not have existed. Daddy said that help arrived just in time. He lay in his blood for what seemed like fifteen or twenty minutes and was beginning to lose consciousness. Paramedics said another two minutes and he could have died.

I wish I could tell you that was the first and last time Daddy had a near-death experience. Daddy shared stories with his friends all the time about how he escaped death. He claimed to even have seen God on one occasion. During that experience he had with God, he claimed he told God that if he would spare his life, he would live his life giving with no regrets or limits. Daddy could not do any wrong in my eyes. He lived a rich life and kept his promise to God, living life giving, serving others, and spreading the good news of Jesus. That's how he met Mama.

During a pastor's anniversary at the church Mama and Great-Grandma Sallie attended, Daddy was visiting on behalf of the guest pastor. He went up to the pulpit to introduce the guest pastor, and I'm told the delivery and introduction he gave was a powerful time in the Lord. It had the church on fire and excited to receive the word of God. After the service, Mama was responsible for serving the pastoral staff in the back. Daddy sat at the table with the pastors, guest pastors, deacons, and elders of the church. When Mama came to their table to serve them a refill of sweet tea, Daddy laid eyes on her and instantly heard from God that she was his wife. Their courtship was short, and their marriage was long.

Daddy was very friendly and compassionate. It was easy to communicate with him and easy for him to share advice and life lessons. It was easy to earn his trust, and he had the respect of everyone in the community. It was not like Daddy to walk around with a closed lip. When Mama was pregnant with their first child, everyone in the entire town knew about it. He celebrated each of her pregnancies the same way. He was not so good at grieving though. When Mama suffered the loss of the two babies birthed between me and my older brother, Daddy lost faith in God. He stopped going to church every Sunday and accused Mama of stealing his money and giving it to another man. He resented the pastor because he thought she loved the pastor more than him. He even drank beer again. Daddy was in a dark place. Neither he nor Mama ever dealt with the passing of those children. They spent a lot of time apart; she spent more time at church and serving the Lord, while Daddy stayed away from church caught up in his insecurities.

When Mama and Daddy found out they were pregnant with me, they were very skeptical. Daddy made another promise to God that if He allowed this baby to be born and survive; he would clean his life back up. Sure enough, God granted his prayers. Mama, however, was still a wreck. Daddy said, "You worry too much, woman! Sit down and rest."

Mama dealt with a crisis by keeping busy. Daddy, however, made deals with the Lord and gained confidence that because he was giving something to the Lord, the Lord would give something back to him. My birth literally saved their marriage and restored their hope and happiness. Daddy was back to his old self again, very laid back. He was the calm in the eye of a storm.

He always taught me to stand up for what I believed in, to speak up for myself, and to follow my dreams. He taught me that how you treat yourself is the blueprint for how others will treat you. Everyone in the community knew how much my daddy loved me and treated me like his special princess. He was very motivational when it came to that type of stuff. He was a hard-working man and set a goal of celebrating his retirement with a fancy black Cadillac with chrome finish. He posted magazine pictures all in the garage to remind him of his goal.

Daddy worked at the factory warehouse for nearly eighteen years. One day, the factory closed down without warning and moved to Colorado. The boss man told Daddy if he wanted to keep his job, then he would need to move to Colorado with the company. How else would Daddy provide for his family? Without a second thought, he came home and told Mama that we were moving to Colorado.

Mama felt that it was not best for our family right then. With a teenager and pre-teen children, being thousands of miles away from home, family, friends, and the church was not beneficial. She said she was not moving, and that was that. Daddy loved Mama very much and hated to be at odds with her, but he really felt in his heart that moving to Colorado was the answer to the family's financial crisis. Daddy told his boss man that he needed more time to finalize some loose ends in South Carolina. He assured him that once things were finalized, he and the family were coming. What he was actually doing was buying more time for Mama to get on the same page.

Days turned into weeks, and weeks turned into months. Daddy still had not gone back to work. The household was struggling. My older brother had to perform odd jobs after school to help bring money into the house. Mama was cleaning bathrooms, knitting, and sewing to bring in what she could, and Daddy was offering his service as a mechanic, performing oil changes and simple mechanical fixes to bring money into the house. I didn't know how to cook or clean, because Mama and Daddy thought it was a crime for me to lift a finger around the house. However, I offered to learn so I could pitch in and pull my weight around the house. Both of them insisted that I continue to enjoy my childhood, make good grades in school, and enjoy my friends.

At night, the arguments grew worse and worse. Erica and Jan moving into the house made things even worse for our family financially. But, Uncle James agreed to send money to Mama and Daddy every month for taking them in. With things between Mama and Daddy getting worse by the day, there was no way I could share with them what had happened between me and Mr. Lawrence.

One day, I came home from school and Daddy was waiting for me on the porch. As I walked up to the house, I saw his car filled with belongings.

"Daddy, are you going somewhere?" I asked.

"Sit down, baby girl. I have to tell you something." I did not like the tone in Daddy's voice. I could tell this was a very serious conversation he was getting ready to have.

"Your mama and I are not seeing eye-to-eye right now, and we agreed that it is best that I move out."

"But where are you going to go, Daddy? Who is going to protect and take care of us?"

"Don't worry about that. Your brother, Junior, is becoming a man now, and he's in charge. I'm not going to be gone for long. This is just some time apart, so your mama and I can get back on the same page."

That day was one of the worst days of my life. I cried and screamed like I was at a funeral. "Daddy, please don't go. Please! I will do anything, Daddy! Please don't go!" I gave him the tightest hug I could.

By that time, Mama came out of the house and told me to wash up for a snack. I was so devastated I didn't feel like eating. Instead, I climbed on the top of Daddy's car, stomping and kicking. It was my goal to damage his car enough that he could not drive it. Daddy assured me that I was the most important person in his world, and he would never leave me. Moving out was just temporary until he and Mama could sort some things out. Daddy picked me up and carried me to the porch.

I looked at Mama and told her, "This is all your fault! If something happens to us, it will be all your fault!"

Chapter 5

FAMILY SECRETS

Daddy and Mama Jones were well-known in the community. When they split, the entire community was impacted by their separation. Sometimes Daddy came to visit, but sometimes he spent weeks away from us like we never existed to him. When he visited, he stayed until I fell asleep. Sometimes I prayed to God that when I woke up Daddy would be there, and we would be a family again.

One random evening after school, Daddy waited for me at the corner store. "Hey, baby girl! I'm here to pick you up, so you can spend the day with me!"

"Does Mama know?"

"Of course, she knows! Hop in and let's go for some ice cream!" Daddy was in a very good mood that day. After a short drive, we arrived at an apartment complex.

"Where are we?" I asked.

"This is my new place! I wanted to show you your room so that you can come and spend the night whenever you want." The distance between Mama's house and Daddy's apartment was very short. I could ride my bike with Erica and Jan here if I wanted to.

When we got to his apartment, he started calling for someone. "Julius! Julius, come here! I want you to meet someone!" A woman came out of the room. She was tall, slender, younger, very light-skinned, and had a huge afro.

"Who is this woman?"

"Rhonda, this is Julius. Julius, Rhonda." Julius leaned over to shake my hand, but I could tell she was not very pleased with my presence, so I kept my hands folded in my arms.

"Daddy, this is grossing me out. Is Julius your girlfriend? Married people don't have girlfriends. Take me home to my mama right now!"

Daddy was embarrassed and apologized to Julius for my behavior. I did not care what Julius thought of me. As far as I knew, my daddy was still a married man, and I was not interested in having a stepmother who was old enough to be my big sister. Julius was still interested in trying to complete my father's agenda.

"Rhonda, why don't you stay for dinner? I know you must be hungry after a long day at school. Your dad told me your favorite meal is lasagna, and I made it just the way you like it, with garlic toast and sweet tea and your favorite dessert, lemon pound cake."

Since I was hungry, I took Julius up on her offer to stay for dinner. But, I made very little eye contact with her and refused to finish my food. When I had enough to eat, I slammed the plate on the floor and told Julius that Mama's lasagna tasted better, and I waited in the car until Daddy came out of the house. He did his best to make me feel welcomed and loved, but I was not having it. I felt blindsided. How could he just bring me to another woman's house without my approval? How could he leave his family like this? He had his nerve.

Later that evening when I returned home, Mama sat at the kitchen table. I was unsure if I should tell her about Julius or if she already knew. Mama was putting the finishing touches on a yellow cake with chocolate frosting.

"I heard you had dinner at your father's house, so I figured I would make you dessert." Since Daddy's move months ago, Mama seemed unbothered about the entire ordeal. My older brother, Junior, had gotten a job at a local grocery store. Mama was still completing odd jobs to support the family, and things went on as normal as if Daddy no longer mattered. I thought I would never see the day that my parents separated or got divorced. I did not want to hurt Mama's feelings about Julius, but something told me she already knew.

One night, I was very sick. My temperature was really high, and Mama was scared. I rarely got sick. Mama panicked and didn't know what to do, so she phoned Daddy. She always believed that a man should take care of a woman, take care of the household, protect, provide, and care for his family. She believed that the woman should be the homemaker and the caretaker of the house. Because I had never gotten sick before, she did not know what was wrong. My daddy rushed over in the middle of the night without a thought.

"I got here as soon as I could, baby girl." He brought a box of popsicles and placed a cool damp cloth over my forehead. Mama and Daddy stayed at my bedside the entire night, praying away this sickness and watching and waiting.

My illness continued into the next day. My throat was sore, and I vomited blood everywhere. Mama and Daddy decided it was time to take me to the emergency room. After several tests and procedures, they could not find out what was wrong with me. The emergency room doctors told my parents to take me to my family doctor first thing in the morning.

Dr. Stokes had been treating our family for years, since before I was born. He delivered Junior, treated my mom for the flu, and treated my dad for his illness. Dr. Stokes ran several tests, and he also concluded that he could not find anything wrong with me.

Dr. Stokes wanted to know if there were any changes in the home. Mama and Daddy looked at each other and responded at the same time. Mama said yes, but Daddy said no. Daddy then told Dr. Stokes that he and Mama had separated and had lived apart for almost a year. Dr. Stokes believed I was having a hard time adjusting to the new normal and suggested that Mama and Daddy try to send me to someone to talk about my problems.

Daddy asked, "You mean a shrink? My baby's not crazy; she is sick!"

Mama added, "Thanks for your time, Doctor, but we will figure things out from here."

They say God works in mysterious ways, and apparently, He allowed my sickness to bring my mama and daddy back together again. When I woke up the next day, all of his things were out of Julius' home and back into our house.

Because there was so much land surrounding the house, Daddy thought it would be a good idea to rent out lots so it could bring some extra income into the home. Junior was a rising senior in high school, and Daddy wanted him to quit working, so he could focus on getting good grades and go to college. He announced to the church that he had mobile home lots for rent and would be taking tenants. Soon, we had our first land tenants; Gerald and his mom, Ebanee.

Gerald and I were around the same age. We were both in junior high school and would sometimes teach Sunday school to the toddlers at church. We formed a pretty good bond as cousins. We shared Bible lessons and sometimes met up to coordinate our lesson plans. Summertime was quickly approaching and Case, Jan,

Veronica Tucker

and Erica would soon be spending time with their father in Germany. Uncle James had already bought plane tickets for them, and they were excited to see what Germany looked like.

That summer, Gerald and I spent a lot of time pretending to have church. Gerald was the preacher, and I pretended to be the congregation, sending up praises and shouting. We loved reading our Bibles, and we bonded in ways that I hadn't with Erica and Jan. At school, we passed each other in the hallway and sometimes had lunch together. Gerald knew I loved to read books, so he purchased books from our school book-fair and gifted them to me.

He did not know who his father was, but he grew up to be a very well-mannered man. Rumor had it that Ebanee was either raped or had gotten pregnant by a married man. Who knows? Our family had lots of secrets, and it was not uncommon to be left out of the loop. It seemed as if everyone was keeping secrets from each other, and nobody was able to answer any questions when I asked. We had not discovered what happened to the children Daddy had with Annie.

The children kept secrets from the adults, and the adults kept secrets from the children. Gerald longed to have a father figure in his life. Daddy did his best, involving Gerald in manly activities, such as changing the oil on the car or cutting the grass. But he wanted a relationship with his own father. I felt bad that he did not know who his father was, or share that bond I had with my daddy. He begged Ebanee to tell him who his father was, but you could tell she was not ready to talk about the events surrounding her pregnancy or who his father was. She retaliated by accusing Gerald of not being grateful for the life God had blessed him with.

Ebanee was much older than Jan, Erica, and me. She babysat us a few times when we were younger, but she

40

appeared to be a mean-spirited person. She always had a man in her life. She always seemed to pick guys who were trouble. Every boyfriend she ended up with only fought and argued with her.

One night, Gerald sensed something was not right, so he hung out a little later after school. He claimed to be hanging out with his friends. Ebanee was in a horrible mood that night. Empty liquor bottles were all about on the floor. When he came in the house, out of nowhere, *wham*! She smashed a Coke bottle over Gerald's head. Shards of glass were stuck in his head, and his face was scratched badly. He left the house yelling and screaming all the way to our house. Ebanee followed.

Mama and Daddy heard the ruckus and met Gerald outside.

"What is going on?" Daddy asked. We were all so afraid that Ebanee was going to kill Gerald. It was as if Ebanee was possessed by something. Mama ran to Gerald's aid with some alcohol and gauze pads to clean him up. Luckily for Gerald, the glass was not deep, and he did not need stitches.

As Mama patched up his head and face, he questioned Ebanee, "Why do you hate me so much? What have I ever done to you?"

Ebanee replied, "I hate you! Since the day you were born, my life has been cursed! I wish you were never born!" Daddy interrupted Ebanee and tried to calm her down. She was still trying to attack Gerald as Mama tried to patch him up.

I got tired of them fighting and yelling, so I told Gerald, "Run, Gerald! Run!" I remember praying to God to please protect him. Ebanee was so enraged. I think if she got close enough to him, she would have killed him. Gerald ran and hid, and I went inside to call the police. Mama insisted that if the police got involved, Ebanee would go to jail. It seemed that the word jail was the key to calming her down. She went back to her mobile home, and Gerald came out of hiding. From that night on, he stayed with us, along with Jan, Erica, and Case.

The next morning, our family carried on like nothing happened the night before. That was the one thing I noticed about our family that somewhat bothered me. We never talked about problems and resolved conflicts. We just moved on from the event or episode as if nothing happened. Even when Mama and Daddy separated, Daddy just moved back into the house as if nothing ever happened! Mama got back into her routine, and Daddy got back into his.

The same thing applied to Daddy and Annie and the children they had. He never discussed them or his family in Atlanta. What was he hiding from us? And why did Mama always appear to be unbothered by anything in life? She rarely raised her voice and rarely showed any emotions. The only way you had any idea something bothered her was when she would get extra busy around the house. She would be going and going like the Energizer Bunny.

And what about the family in the photo with Uncle James? Who were they? Why did we not know anything about them? Why did Case, Jan, and Erica's mommy never come around the family? I had so many unanswered questions about what went on in our family. Even when I became a teenager, I was told to stay in a child's place. But, it seemed like the adults around me were the ones acting like children.

A few weeks after Gerald and Ebanee's brawl, he appeared to be getting settled in at our place. One day, I came home from school tired and really felt like a nap. I did not expect anyone to be home. Jan and Erica stayed after school for tutoring. Daddy worked, and Mama was out running errands. I heard a noise coming from the living room and grew curious. I was spooked, so I picked up a kitchen knife in case I had to protect myself. When I entered the living area, to my surprise, Gerald and Rosa were on the couch making out. Rosa attended the same junior high school I did. I had no idea that she and Gerald were dating.

"Hey, Rosa. What are you doing here?"

"I live here now!" I was surprised.

"Rosa, who gave you permission to live here? This is my parents' home. They did not make me aware that you were living here now!" Gerald joined in on the conversation.

"Rhonda, listen. I will be graduating high school soon and plan to enter the military. Rosa might be pregnant, and her parents kicked her out of the house. I just need a safe space for her to lay low until graduation in a few more weeks. Please, Rhonda. Please keep this secret for us!"

I knew right then I did not like Rosa or what she represented. I felt she was taking advantage of Gerald because he was going to the military soon. We all knew Gerald was in a vulnerable place because of the relationship with his mom and the lack of a relationship with his father. He always wanted a family and to feel like he belonged, and Rosa took advantage of that. She had her way with the boys. She was very fast and sexually mature for her age. I felt like Gerald could have picked a better girlfriend. Therefore, I did not agree to keep his secret from Mama and Daddy. He was on his own. He got a job and worked very hard to provide for himself while finishing up high school.

When Gerald graduated, he shared with the family that Rosa was pregnant, and he was going to the military so that he could provide for his family. He graduated at seventeen, but required permission to enter the military.

To our surprise, Ebanee signed the papers! She declared, "He is someone else's problem now." Ebanee was still Ebanee. Nothing had changed since the night of the fight.

That following Monday, Rosa and Gerald sat with the family appearing to be very happy and giddy.

I asked, "Rosa, what are you doing here?"

"What does it look like I am doing, Rhonda? I'm sitting with my husband."

"Excuse me. Your husband? Since when? You're not even old enough to get married."

Rosa explained that because she was pregnant, her parents signed off on the papers for her to get married. I felt Gerald was making a horrible mistake, but who was I to tell him this? He was excited about showing me his marriage certificate and did his best to reassure me that he was doing the right thing. There was something not right about Rosa and Gerald, and I was going to make it my priority to get to the bottom of it.

Emotional Murder

Chapter 6

JONATHAN ROBERTSON
Mistaken Identity of First Love

I realized there wasn't much I could do about Gerald and Rosa, since they had gotten their own apartment. Erica, Jane, and Case had gone to Japan with their dad. We weren't having our family dinners as often as we used to. Momma and Daddy appeared to be okay, I was glad about Daddy being back home, but I was missing everyone, and the fun we all had together. I love being a giver of love and expressly enjoyed when it was reciprocated. I learned the hard way the love you give don't necessarily return back to you. Our first love is an important experience that holds so many lessons. For me, the first lesson of first love was the mistaken identity of your first love. A *first love* means a love that comes before all others: the greatest love, greater than our love for ourselves, family, and friends. I had to be taught first love is Christ himself, who loved you before you were formed in your mother's womb. The first love for Christ drives us to seek to be conformed to His image and learn to act and react as He would. You often will leave your first love, but your first love will never leave you.

No matter what age, a first romance has an innocent, earnest sense of discovery, and exploration. I remember mine like yesterday. I decided to sneak outside to the candy lady's house, and right next door, there was a bunch of children from the neighborhood playing dodgeball. I rarely saw the children from the neighborhood outside of school.

One of the kids yelled, "Hey, Rhonda, we need another person on our team." I thought to myself, *sure why not*? Mama was on the phone with her cousin, Lily Mae. They were more like sisters and would talk for hours, so I knew Mama wouldn't miss me.

I decided to go over and play with the other children. The objective of dodgeball is to eliminate all players of the opposing team by throwing one of four game balls and hitting the opposing player. As I tried to avoid getting hit, I looked up and Jonathan Robertson was throwing the ball to me. He was almost six feet tall at the age of twelve. He had broad shoulders and reddish-brown, coily-curly hair, sweat dripping down his small nose. His golden skin, thick, defined eyebrows, and light brown eyes, caught my full attention. He was very handsome and I had never seen a black boy who looked like him. He had freckles on his face; he also had them all over his hands and arms.

I continued looking at every inch of this boy, and the ball came flying right at me. I forgot all about dodging the ball, I tried to catch it. My index finger bent backwards. I screamed. "Oh my God! It hurts!"

Jonathan ran up to me and asked, "Hey, are you alright? You're supposed to dodge the ball, not catch it." He continued to laugh; it was cute, but definitely not funny. I looked at him and rolled my eyes.

He responded, "I'm just playing."

I tried to shake the pain off, while backing up and walking out of the yard. I figured hurting my finger was a sign that I shouldn't have sneaked out of the house anyway. I turned around and this freckled-face boy was following me down the street on a blue and yellow bike.

He asked, "Hey, what's your name? I've never seen you before."

"Rhonda."

"My name is Jonathan, but I go by Jay. Are you hurt bad? Come on, stay. Be on my team."

"None of your business. Why are you following me?"

"I think you're pretty, and I wanted to talk to you."

"Oh, well. I have to go home."

"Let me give you a kiss goodbye then."

"That's gross. You are not putting your lips on me, boy!"

"Come on now. Kissing is not gross."

"Go back and finish playing your little game."

"Hey, I'm spending the night at my aunt's house if you change your mind."

I made it to our house, still holding my finger. I ran right into Mama.

She gave me a stern look, and I said, "I was just sitting on the porch." Mama was still on the phone. She was so deep in conversation; she didn't even ask how I hurt my finger. She grabbed a washcloth, filled it with ice, told me to sit, and put the ice on my finger.

Summer was ending, and I was happy about going back to school and meeting some new friends. I remember Erica talking about how middle school was, and her bragging how much easier it is to make friends. Middle school started, I was looking forward to more freedom and making friends. I was always very friendly. Mama would say "too friendly." I noticed a lot of the girls got a lot of attention because they had big breasts and behinds. I even overheard some them talking about how they were having sex. So far, I had nothing in common with any of them.

I didn't know anything about sex, besides what I saw in the magazines I found in the basement of our home. I didn't discuss sex with my parents. Well, at least not in a manner in which I understood the process. I was pretty much naïve about the whole thing. I remember the brief discussion Mama had with me made me more fearful than informative. Once I got my menstrual cycle, Mama said, "So, you got your period. You're a young lady now. No, more my little baby." She gave me the look, told me to go get the Bible.

Mama said, "See, this book is going to tell you how a woman is supposed to act. Only married adults have sex. Unmarried women that have sex, go to hell."

She said, "A period means you can have a baby. Sex and babies before marriage are a sin, and you will burn in hell."

She turned to 1 Corinthians 6:18-20 in the Bible.

"Flee sexual immorality. Every sin that a man does is outside the body, but he who commits sexual immorality sins against his own body. Or do you not know that your body is the temple of the Holy Spirit who is in you, whom you have from God, and you are not your own?

For you were bought at a price; therefore, glorify God in your body [a]and in your spirit, which are God's."

After she finished reading it aloud, she made me read it too. She closed the Bible and placed it back under her pillow, and gave me a look of assurance that I got the picture.

That same weekend, Daddy took me to breakfast. He said, "Mama told me you're a young lady now. You'll always be my baby girl."

I felt very relieved. I loved being his baby girl and had no interest in having sex or babies. Ew...gross. Especially, if it meant I was going to burn in hell.

Daddy said, "Take your time and don't rush into anything. I know your mama tried to scare you, talking about you going to hell. If that was the case, she and I would already be there. The main thing is love and affection. Love is the best part of sex. Cooking meals and paying bills is not affection."

At that point, I wasn't sure who or what Daddy was talking about. The waitress brought over my buttered grits, scrambled eggs, fried flounder, and jelly toast.

Daddy only had coffee, and I noticed he hadn't been eating much and had lost a lot of weight. Daddy said he enjoyed seeing me eat, especially after I went through the phase of not eating and being underweight. Daddy was the best; hanging with him meant everything in the world to me.

I learned how to asked Daddy for permission for everything because I knew the answer was always going to be yes.

I asked permission to go to the ball games at the park a few blocks from where we lived. I remember walking to the park for the first time, we heard all the people yelling before turning the corner. We stopped on the side where vendors were selling hot dogs, chips, and candy. I was only allowed to eat candy on holidays. I bought a bunch of Now and Later. Before we got to the stands to watch the baseball game, we noticed this one kid, number eleven, continuously hitting the ball over the fence, scoring a hit and run each time. I could barely see his face, but I recognized those eyes.

Jonathan ran the bases. He looked over in the stands, winking his eye and said, "I see you came looking for me."

I thought, *this boy is really full of himself.* A bunch of girls called his name like he was the only player on the field.

He appeared to know just about everyone from his neighborhood and ours. He played baseball and football at the field near our house. Each game, he scored more than any of the other players on both teams, but I didn't let him know I noticed. It seemed as if Jonathan was popping up everywhere.

At our school we would have these dances, called the "Hop." Children from other schools came to the dances at my school, we had dance contests. Jonathan was apparently a good dancer as well. It was a seventh-grade Hop and I remember walking into the gym. Everyone was crowded around watching this kid dance to Michael Jackson's "Beat It." He had on the Michael Jackson jacket, leather pants, glove, glittery socks, and black loafers. He threw his black hat off as he finished the dance. All the girls screamed and hollered like he was really Michael Jackson. I locked eyes with light brown eyes, and it was Jonathan. At this point, I was pretty much grossed out with all boys, so it didn't bother me that the boys didn't pay me much attention. I still thought kissing was disgusting, and the thought of exchanging saliva with another human being made my stomach ball up in knots. Nevertheless, I wasn't grossed out by Jonathan, but I was annoyed by his arrogant attitude.

He came over and said, "Hey, do you see how I came to your school and won the dance contest? I am the best you ever laid eyes on, girl."

"Oh, please. Whatever. You all right."

"All right? I taught Michael Jackson everything he know, girl."

He started dancing and doing a spin. I laughed. "So, I guess you're a comedian too."

"I could be if I wanted to. I can be anything I want. I used to think that I could have anything I wanted, but you're around here playing hard to get."

"You're just a boy. You shouldn't be worried about getting anybody."

"Girl, please. My Uncle Darius told me I was a young man now, and he taught me everything I know about how to love on the ladies."

A group of girls came over pulling him away, so he could dance with them, he let them drag him away, but as he was leaving, he said, "Stop being so mean with your pretty self. You'll be mine one day soon."

I just rolled my eyes and thought I had to give it to Jonathan for his persistence.

I really enjoyed middle school, in spite of not having much in common with the other children. I loved my teachers, and I loved learning new things. It seemed as if eighth grade had arrived much too soon. I wasn't ready for high school. The thought of going to high school was a little scary to me, so I decided to enjoy the last bit of middle school as much as I could. I made sure I didn't miss any basketball games, since that was the only sport I understood. Our basketball team, the Eagles, made it to the playoffs.

Heyward Gibbes Middle School vs. St. Andrews Middle School, everyone was talking about the game. Both schools had great players, and the competition was really intense.

Kisha, the niece of our neighbor across the street said she had to be there. Kisha was about three years older than me. She visited on the weekends and sometimes, she would come over and go to the games with me, that was the only reason my parents let me go to the games. She was what we called a "holy girl." She never wore pants and was in church more than Mama and me.

We walked in the gym. The Eagles were on the left, and the Saints were on the right. As the game began and they announced the players, I heard the announcer call out the captain of the team and shooting guard, "Jonathan Robertson." There was a lot of yelling from the stands on both ends. "Go, Jay!"

I noticed a very pretty, slim, middle-aged lady yelling, "That's my baby!" She had freckles too. I had never seen his mom before, but I was pretty certain that was her. In fact, the left side of the gym was his family, classmates, and both cheerleading teams, screaming his name.

The game started, and it looked like the Eagles were winning. The Saints were down the first half of the game. Jonathan was number eleven, and I could see the frustration on his face. He looked like the weight of the team was on his shoulders. The second half of the game, Jonathan appeared as if he really dug himself into a zone, making the score ten to three. Jonathan's coach immediately called timeout. The Saints were hyped because of the comeback. I'm not sure what was said during the timeout, but after the timeout, they scored back to back. The Saints eventually made a run in the fourth to take the lead. Ten seconds were left inside the fourth quarter and Jonathan's coach called another timeout. The coach drew up a play, but Jonathan wasn't even paying attention. It was like he zoned out. I knew he was very competitive and wanted to win. Jonathan stepped back on the court, and not even knowing the play, he moved left wing as they inbounded. As the ball inbounded on two of his teammates on the right, Jonathan immediately ran to the top of the key screaming for the ball. The clock was ticking, and the crowd was counting down. "Seven, six, five, four…" One of his teammates finally threw him the ball, and he caught it and fired it for a quick three-pointer. *Bang!* He hit the game winner. Relief was on his face as his teammates crowded around him.

After each game, it was a struggle to speak to him because he was always surrounded by his fan club. This night in particular, he yelled my name while there were other girls all around him, trying to get his attention. He told me to meet him at his aunt's house. Seeing all those other girls fall over him piqued my curiosity. He could have chosen one of those other girls, but he called for me.

I said in my head, *I am not meeting him anywhere.* Nevertheless, my mouth had a different response. "I yelled back, "Okay, see you in a few!" I really surprised myself. I became very nervous, but it didn't stop me from meeting him.

My daddy drove Kisha and me home. Kisha lived on the other side of town, but she stayed with her aunt, and her aunt would drive her to school the following morning. I told Daddy Jones I was walking her across the street, which I did. When she was at the first step of her aunt's door, I said good night and ran up the street to Jonathan's aunt's house. He was sitting on the porch still in his uniform. First thing I noticed were his light brown eyes and his white teeth. He had a big grin on his face.

"I knew you were coming."

"Oh, you did?" Jonathan was very cocky and very sure of himself. I noticed that when he played sports, he talked plenty of mess, which also had him known as a hot head. Yet, in that very moment, he was suddenly acting shy and quiet. He fixed his socks several times, unbuttoned his jacket about six times, then he asked if he could put his arms around me. I said okay. I wasn't grossed out. My stomach wasn't in knots, but my heart was beating really fast and so was his.

I said, "You sure are quiet all of a sudden."

Jonathan cleared his throat. "Hey, I don't know what it is. You got me nervous. I should have taken a shower. I'm so sweaty. I don't want to be stinking around you."

He got up and grabbed his gym bag. "No, wait! I don't have much time before I have to go home."

He sat back down. I could see the wetness of his uniform, and his forehead was still sweaty.

I was shocked. This boy was this close to me, and I didn't want to vomit or mind that we were so close together. There was dead silence for about two minutes. He put his arm around me again. Sweat was supposed to make you stink, but that sure wasn't the case for Jonathan. I smelled a strong, masculine fragrance, Halston cologne. I laid my head on his chest, and his heart was still beating very fast.

I looked up, and he kissed me. I felt as if my whole body was flaming with fire. I allowed this teenage boy to put his tongue down my throat, and it felt nice. I could tell Jay had done this before. He knew exactly how to position my head to go for the kiss.

Daddy often told me how beautiful I am. He always treated me like I was the best thing that ever happened to him. When Jay told me these things, it felt different. After all, he was one of the most popular boys around, and he was absolutely gorgeous.

"I have to get back home."

He said, "I want to see you again. Give me your phone number."

I knew it wasn't going to be easy, because I wasn't allowed to have boys calling me yet. Jonathan tried calling me a few times, but Mama would hang up in his face and say, "Rhonda can't get any calls from boys yet."

After this went on for a few months, Jonathan stopped calling. It seemed as if I could never catch up with him at his aunt's house.

The summer before high school, I learned from Jonathan's cousin, Kenya that he was staying with his cousins, Alberta, Kenya, and Charles for the summer at his Aunt Fern's house. Kenya didn't give me much detail at the time, she just said that his mother was sick and he would be with them for the whole summer, and maybe part of the school year. I was so excited about seeing Jonathan. I prayed he would not be upset that I was not able to talk on the phone with him since Mama was so strict. I saw Jonathan sitting in the front yard with his baseball uniform on, smiling like he was glad to see me too. We had not seen each other since our first kiss, so we had a very long embrace. That hug lit up my whole body. We sat on his aunt's front porch, holding hands and talking.

I learned that he loved sports in general, but his passion was basketball. He was an only child and didn't talk much about his father. Jonathan was always smiling, and he loved joking around. One time I recalled seeing him upset when he talked about his father. His father was supposed to buy him some new basketball shoes, and bring them before his game, but his father never showed up. He said, "I hate that man. He means nothing to me. I never want to be anything like him." At that point, as far as I could tell, Jonathan was nothing like his father. Jonathan was very compassionate and thoughtful.

Jay appeared very close to his mother. I remember him writing her letters, and asking God to heal his mother. I was told by his cousin, Alberta, that Jonathan was his mother's golden child, and he could do no wrong in her eyes.

I could tell Jay was used to getting his way at home and anywhere else. I could tell he had his way even while staying with his Aunt Fern. He never missed any games, and he was always at practice. I enjoyed walking to the park with Jonathan; he was just as good in baseball as basketball. Mama would never let me miss church, so I missed some of the games. When we met up at his aunt's house after games, he would reenact all his best moments of the game. I loved school, but I also didn't like when the summer ended.

After the summer, Jonathan's mother came to his aunt's house and he went back home with her. I was a bit sad because I was looking forward to us going to the same school, but I was happy for Jonathan because he missed his mother a lot.

I continued to be nervous about high school. I particularly didn't want to go to the school I was zoned for. I heard some horror stories about girls being raped in the bathroom and fights breaking out every day. I begged Mama to let me go to another school, but it didn't work.

School was back in about a month, and only one fight had broken out in the hallway. It didn't seem so bad. Jonathan and I talked almost every day, some weekdays he would sneak in my room and we would study. He was very smart and attended advanced classes. He worked hard to keep up his grades, since it was the only way his mother would allow him to play all the sports he wanted. It was kind of cool to have such a popular boyfriend.

I also quickly learned the consequences of Jonathan's popularity. One morning, I entered at the back of the school. Five girls were standing to the side of the wall. I noticed one of the girls, LaShawn, who hung out at Jonathan's aunt's house with his cousins.

I said hello.

She said, "Bitch, don't speak to me."

I was shocked because she didn't appear to be mean and rude before.

LaShawn said, "I saw JR last night, and his lips were so soft."

I didn't say anything. I kept walking. LaShawn and her friends started to follow me.

LaShawn yelled, "Hey you, do you hear me? JR is mine, so you need to stay away from him."

I continued to ignore them, so I kept walking.

"So, you too good to speak?" LaShawn ran in front of me, and her friends were on each side of her. "Did you hear what I said, hoe? Jonathan is my man, and I was with him last night."

I finally spoke, "Oh really? It's funny that you say you were with him last night. He must have a twin because he was in my room last night lying on my bed helping me study for a math quiz."

LaShawn friend's response was "Ooh...I guess she told you."

LaShawn was six feet one, in the ninth grade, she was kept back multiple times so I had no idea how old she was, but she had nails like a cougar. She said, "Okay, I got you, you stuck-up hoe. Let's see what you have to say tomorrow."

I was so relieved when they stopped following me. I couldn't wait to get home and confront Jonathan about LaShawn. When I got off the bus, Jonathan was on the side of our house at the picnic table.

I said, "What are you doing here?"

"I came to see you, beautiful."

"So, you didn't have school today?"

"Yes, I did. I got out early."

"Jonathan, who is LaShawn to you?"

"What's up with all the questions? Aren't you glad to see me?"

Jonathan pulled me to him, kissing me on the lips to keep me from talking.

I pulled away and pushed him. "Listen, I saw her today, and she was warning me to stay away from you, talking about she was with you last night."

"Well, you know that was a lie. I was with you last night. Listen, she likes me. She is always writing me letters, and she shows up at my cousin's house when I am there. But, I don't want her. She is a ghetto girl. I like a church girl, you know a good girl, like you."

Jonathan had a huge grin on his face. "You like church girls, huh? Yet, you always trying to have sex."

"I love you." That was the first time Jonathan said that he loved me.

Those eyes had me in a trance. I looked in his eyes thinking how much I might love him too.

"I must love you, because you haven't given me none yet, and I'm still around."

"Given you none? None of what?"

He pulled me closer, kissing me on my neck. "You know exactly what I talking about."

"Look, I told you I'm not having sex with someone who isn't my husband."

"Hey, we can't get married now, but just wait until I get into the NBA. You're going to be my wife."

"Yeah, right. You'll probably will forget all about me."

"No. Look, we're going to live large. I'm going to have a bunch of cars, and you can have a boy first. I can teach him how to play sports. Our second child will be a girl, and I'll be her hero. See, girl, you need to stop holding back. I will be your husband."

"Since you already know I'm a church girl, let me pray about it and get back with you."

Daddy drove up.

Jonathan said, "Hey, I'm going to see you later."

He knew how strict my parents were, and he said he'd rather not meet them. It was too late for Jonathan to run away. Daddy was already out of the car coming towards us.

"Baby girl, who is this?"

"Daddy, this is Jonathan."

"Hey, sir, how are you doing?"

"Hey, I saw you on the front page of the newspaper. You're doing big things on the court."

"Yes sir."

"All right, baby, stay out a few minutes longer and come on in."

"I thought your dad was going to curse me out. He's actually a cool dude."

"Yes, my daddy's the best on the planet."

"I bet he has you so spoiled."

"Yes, and you know this."

"I got practice, so I'll see you later. Think about what I said."

I decided to wear my favorite gold necklace and ring. My mama gave it to me. Her grandma gave it to her. It belonged to my grandma's mother, who she never knew. I loved jewelry, and Daddy and Mama made sure I had a lot of it. I rarely wore dresses anymore, but I had a t-shirt that was spray painted with "Jonathan N Rhonda" on the back. This was very stylish at the time. I even had the bullet-toe Nikes with our names on the side. I arrived at school, and the same five girls were standing on the wall. I tried to walk by, but they formed a circle around me. They started to push me, one by one.

"What you got to say now?"

"We're about to whip your ass, you conceited heifer."

"You think you look good with your little new dress. We're about to tear that little dress off of you, hoe."

One of them pushed me so hard that I fell and hit my head on the cement. I don't remember much after that. I was told my nephew, Calvin, and his friends heard about the fight. They rushed me and pulled the girls off. I woke up in the ER. All of my jewelry was gone, and my dress was covered in blood and ripped.

My head was hurting so bad. "What happened?"

Daddy said, "You were jumped by some hoodrats because of that funny-looking boy you like so much."

"Daddy, why are you calling him funny-looking?"

"There aren't any black people walking around with freckles all over their bodies."

"His grandmother is white. I guess it runs in the family."

"I don't care where it runs. I don't want that boy around my house. If it wasn't for him, this never would've happened. Look at your face."

I looked in the mirror, and my eye was black and purple and swollen. I could barely see out of it. Jonathan's cousin, Alberta, walked in the room. "Hey, girl, Jay sent me to check on you."

"Why didn't he come himself?"

"Girl, you know your daddy doesn't like him. They said your daddy went looking for him afterwards."

Daddy came back into the room after getting me some water. "You're right. I don't. At least the boy got sense enough not to come up here."

"Daddy, really? You met him the other day, and you liked him."

"I never said that, and just because I didn't kick his funny-looking self out of my yard, doesn't mean I like him."

The police came into the room with Principal Woods. The officer said, "We are here to get a statement from you about the assault."

Principal Woods said, "Listen, I understand your jewelry was stolen. I know you've been through a lot, but I'm here on behalf of LaShawn and her mother."

"Mr. and Mrs. Jones, I just want you and your daughter to consider that LaShawn comes from a low-income family, and they can't afford bail money or to pay for the jewelry that was taken."

Daddy screamed, "What?" He jumped out of his seat, charging toward Principal Woods.

The police officer said, "Sir, if you don't calm down, you'll be arrested."

"Daddy, Daddy, stop. I don't want you to go to jail."

I stood up but fell down to the floor. I couldn't take this. I was literally sick to my stomach. I started vomiting, and everyone left except my parents.

While I was in the bathroom, I heard Daddy carrying on, talking about he'd better not catch "that funny-looking boy" back at his house.

Jonathan doesn't like confrontation unless he is the antagonist. So, I knew he wouldn't try to call or come around. Daddy and Mama were watching me like a hawk, screening my calls and making sure that I didn't make my way up the street to Jonathan's aunt's house.

I felt some type of way that Jonathan never tried to make a way to see me.

I went back to school after a week. I begged Mama to send me to another school. It was awkward returning to school after what happened, I thought to myself, if I could get through the day, I might be okay. LaShawn and her friends continued with their taunting. I just ignored them. One day, I tried to get to my homeroom early, so I wouldn't run into them in the hall. I heard someone say hello. It was Jonathan's cousin, Kynlee. Jonathan had a huge family, so he had cousins at every school in South Carolina.

"Hey, girl. What are you doing here?"

She said, "I go here now."

"Have you heard anything from your cousin, Jonathan?"

"Girl, you know Uncle Darius died."

"No, I didn't know. He was the only father figure to Jonathan, so he must be messed up right now."

"Yeah, girl. I just saw Jonathan at my auntie's house the other day. He is not handling it well. He is in some serious trouble. You just may want to leave him alone. Rhonda, I don't know what you see in him. I thought you were one of those quiet types, a church girl. I heard you're around here taking off your clothes and everything following after him."

"Oh, my goodness! I didn't take my clothes off; those ghetto girls tore my dress off because it had Jonathan's and my name on it."

"Jonathan has gotten himself into something that he can't get out of. Just forget about him. He is really messed up right now. You better off."

"What do you mean, Kynlee?"

"You'll find out soon enough. I'll talk to you later. I have to go to class."

I replied, "Maybe we can get together after school."

"No, I have to go to work. I don't have a mama and daddy taking care of me. I have to buy my own clothes and whatever else I need."

"Where do you work?"

"I work at the Burger King down by the USC campus. You should come down and apply. There are a lot of college guys who come in there. It'll give you something else to do beside think about Jonathan."

I ignored Kynlee's advice about forgetting about Jonathan. I believed Jonathan was the love of my life and no matter what the circumstances were, we would always find our way back to each other. I was not interested in meeting anyone else, but I sure didn't mind having a job, and getting away from Daddy and Mama's little prison.

Even after what happened to me, and my family and the school finding out, LaShawn and her friends continued bullying me. Somehow, they got our home number and called, making threats. LaShawn said, "Next time, you will be knocked out for good." Mama got really upset, and Daddy assured her that they were just trying to scare me, that they didn't want any more trouble. Mama became really strict again, even more than before. I had to go straight home from school up until the eleventh grade. I had a hard time convincing them to let me work. After all, I was sixteen now. It took some time, but I finally convinced them. Daddy took me to the interview and even sat in on the interview. Daddy even answered some of the questions the shift manager was asking me. She even mentioned several times, "I see your father is very overprotective." In my head, I thought, *I am so not getting hired for this job.* To my surprise, at the end of interview, she went to the back to get my uniform. I was so excited about having a job. I was even more excited about using it as a cover-up to see Jonathan.

My soul burned with desire to see Jonathan. This particular Saturday, I told my parents I would be working overtime because of the big game at USC. I worked that day, but not the whole day. That afternoon, I met with Jonathan. It was the first time I saw where he lived. The neighborhood was very rough, but the decor inside was very nice. Jonathan said his mother decorated, and she made a bunch of stuff herself. I was very nervous. I was sure Jonathan could tell. I still had on my coat, hat, and gloves.

Jonathan said, "Let's go in my room." His room had a stereo and posters of Michael Jordan and Tony Dorsett. He was a diehard Cowboys fan. In the corner was a sketchpad full of drawings, and there was even a drawing of me.

"Oh, my goodness! Who drew this?"

"I did."

"So, wait, you are an artist too? Wow! That's amazing."

"I know."

"You are so full of yourself."

He went over to the stereo and played James Ingram's, "One Hundred Ways."

"Hey, you always carrying around that journal. Are you writing about me?"

"Yes, I guess you can say that. I like writing as a hobby. I think I've had a diary as long as I could write."

Jonathan said, "So, you write poems?"

I said, "Something like that. I write what I feel. It's relaxing and very private."

"You can share with me. At least read me the last thing you wrote in there."

I said, "I'm not sure if you want to hear it."

"Yes, I really do. You're always so quiet, so I want to hear what you're thinking."

"Okay, here it is." I took a breath and read, "I look at him as a forbidden fruit, so delicious, so nice, filling my head with beautiful promises, as he entice. I giggle...I blush...I am flush with anticipation yet knowing waiting is a must, I am a lady in waiting. But, looking at him is so inviting. No time to taste. It would be waste if I pick and he not ripe inside, I risk my emotions collide. My desire could bring division, the decision need revision. I cannot stunt my growth, for I had taken an oath. The spirit is willing but the flesh is weak, I must remain virtuous and not eat. No sex before marriage, now back up!"

"Okay, so does it really say that last part?" Jonathan said, "Oh wow, I am a forbidden fruit?"

I said, "I didn't mean as a bad thing."

Jonathan said, "I am good and ripe. I am ready to be picked."

I said, "That's why I didn't want to read it. You taking it too personal."

Jonathan said, "It's about me, that's right, I am taking it personal, it's alright though."

"I am just joking with you. Anyway, I actually want to be a doctor, I hate seeing people sick. I want to be the one that helps them feel better. The only thing is I am not good with math."

"Hey Dr Rhonda Robertson, yeah that sounds good. Math is no problem, I make A's in math, I can help you. I believe you can do anything you set your mind to, you are almost as smart as me."

I realized that Jonathan appeared very interested in my opinion and how I was feeling, when we were together. If he noticed me gazing off, he would ask what I was thinking. He always asked was everything good with me, and that I could talk to him about anything. I really started to imagine myself with him for the rest of my life. After I finished speaking, he turned to me and asked if he could kiss me.

Our clothes were on the floor within a few minutes, and we made our way to the bed. He reached over and turned off the ceiling light, giving the room a warm glow. It was at that moment we both knew it would happen. He asked me if I wanted to make love, I nodded my head in agreement. I felt a million different emotions. He climbed over me and we made eye contact. A moment later, it happened, we had sex for the first time.

It's funny, because I originally considered it the first time we made love, but I later discovered that love cannot be made. Love is not a feeling, it's a decision. As we were in it, the thought crossed my mind, *I can never reverse this*. I wasn't bothered by it, I did not feel taken advantage of, but more astounded I was no longer a virgin.

After we finished, he turned to me and said, "I love you, you are mine forever." I told him, I loved him too. He said, "I love you this much," as he grabbed my arm leading me toward the door. Very comfortable with himself, he jumped fully exposed, while I wrapped the sheet around me. We stood at the front door, he opened it, and I stood behind the door.

He said "Look outside, that how much I love you, more than outdoors." He kissed me on the forehead, we went back to his room, I laid my head on his chest, he wrapped his arms around me, and I fell asleep.

Jonathan mother was rarely home, so we had a lot of alone time together. I felt bad about lying about work, so I did actually work overtime, so it became quite the task keeping up with Jonathan, work and school, I barely had time for church, but of course, Mama was not allowing me to miss church.

Chapter 7

TAKING RESPONSIBILITY

I clearly remembered the excitement, the adrenaline rush, the butterflies, the overwhelming feeling and for the most part, fear. Fear of the unknown, of what shall unfold in the future for Jonathan and me. With emotions bursting inside of me each time we met, I found myself giving in to him each time. Part of me felt really guilty and wondered what type of punishment I would receive from God or Mama, for not saving myself for marriage. I put aside fear, and being unsure when I was in his presence, I just lived in the moment. Which lead to the moment I was dreading.

I walked into the living room, and Mama took one look at me and asked, "Who licked the sugar off your candy?" I sat on the side of her bed and told her I was pregnant.

She said, "You're lying. What's wrong with you, girl? Stop playing like that."

"I'm not lying, Mama. I went to the emergency room because my side was hurting, and they took my urine. The doctor and nurse said I am pregnant." Before

I could get the word pregnant out, she slapped me so hard I had to balance myself to keep from falling off the bed.

"You are not quitting school! You don't have to keep it."

"Mama! Really? I thought you said abortion is not of God."

"Do you want to ruin your life? It's not of God for you to start out like this. You're supposed to go to school."

"Well, I read in the Bible, the same one you read. You do believe what you read, right?"

"You've lost your mind, following behind that boy. What's wrong with you? Why are you having sex anyway? You were supposed to save yourself for marriage."

"Jonathan said we're going to get married one day."

"Oh really? Why in the hell would he marry you now? He got what he wanted. Does he even have a job? Do you know he lives in the projects? Where is his daddy? Girl, you're not keeping this baby."

I couldn't believe that the same lady who dragged me to church every week, always talking about how important it is to take responsibility for your actions, was behaving this way. I knew Mama wouldn't be pleased, but her displeasure didn't mean that much to me at that moment. I imagined myself in a wedding gown holding my bridal bouquet, standing with my back to the people, and then tossing the bridal bouquet. I looked so happy and so peaceful on that day.

Jonathan and I were going to be a family. I prayed it would be a boy like we talked about. I couldn't listen to her hypocritical words anymore. I thought, *I will have this child, and there is nothing she can do about it. He is a gift from God, and I'm going to love him.*

For the first seven and half months of my pregnancy, Daddy had no clue I was pregnant. I assumed Mama would tell him, but she didn't. I started to believe she wanted it to be a form of punishment for me to see the disappointment on his face, considering how close Daddy and I were. I was determined not to face anyone else, and witness the backlash, which included Daddy. I wore very big clothes, and kept a jacket or sweater on most of the time.

I told Jonathan over the phone about the pregnancy, and he claimed he was away at a basketball camp with Michael Jordan. I was doing well at eight months and no one at school knew, except for LaShawn and her crew. I believed Jonathan may have told them. LaShawn caught me in the hall, said that I was lucky I was pregnant. She claimed it saved me from her and her crew bothering me. Fortunately, that was the last time I saw them.

I was still working at Burger King. I remembered watching the college students coming in and how happy they appeared. I was about to be launched into adulthood sooner than expected and wondered if I could still have the college life. I was at work that morning and my supervisor asked if I could work the evening shift. It was midnight and we were about to close. I started to feel bad and had a painful burning sensation in my chest. I was working the drive-thru, taking orders, and the pain got stronger and stronger. I grabbed my chest and slumped to the floor. I had no clue what was happening. I called my dad and asked him if he could come get me from work early. I was still holding my chest. When he got there, I told him what was going on, and he drove me to the emergency room. While checking in, I told the nurse I was pregnant. Once I was placed in a room, my daddy came to the back to be with me.

The ER doctor entered the room.

Daddy said, "Hey, Doctor. She's too young to have a heart attack, right?"

"It's not a heart attack, Mr. Jones. Heartburn is very common in pregnant women."

"Pregnant women? My daughter's not pregnant."

"Mr. Jones, that's what I have on my chart. I'm going to come back in a few minutes and do an ultrasound, just to make sure everything is okay."

The nurse gave me some liquid Maalox. She believed it was heartburn when I first told her I was pregnant. I started to feel better after the Maalox. Once Daddy realized I was actually pregnant, my chest tightened up again.

When the doctor walked out of the room, there was dead silence between Daddy and me until we left the emergency room. "Rhonda, why would you keep this from me? I'm your daddy, and you're my baby girl."

I couldn't say anything, because I really didn't know what to say.

"Is it that funny-looking boy?"

"Yes, sir. It's Jonathan's."

My daddy said, "Don't worry about anything. I'm going to take care of you, just don't ask him or his family for anything. We can handle this."

I was relieved Daddy took it much better than Mama, but was concerned that he didn't want Jonathan nor his family involved.

Mama didn't have much during my pregnancy, but she always had a full-course meal each time I came home from school. She made sure I didn't miss any days of school. Once I went on homebound, she set up the family room like a small classroom, making sure the homebound teacher and I had everything needed to complete school work. Mrs. Smalls was my homebound teacher, and I often heard

Mama asking her did she still think I could go to college. Mrs. Smalls assured Mama I was working hard and that college was always an option, it was up to me.

I remember going into labor around four o'clock in the morning. My daddy drove me to the hospital, and Mama actually came along. She appeared to be excited, but her face didn't reveal any expression. While in labor, there were so many calls coming in from family asking how I was doing.

Mama said, "I don't have a cry baby. My baby girl is handling it like a woman. She's doing good." I was just about to let out a big scream, but I held it in. I felt proud that she believed I was handling it well. Especially after feeling like I let her down by getting pregnant, which haunted me during the entire pregnancy.

I gave birth to my firstborn; a healthy baby boy. I was happy and afraid all at the same time. I was happy to be staring at that gorgeous baby who looked exactly like Jonathan, and I was praying he would be as talented as Jonathan. It was one of the happiest days of my life, except Jonathan wasn't there. I learned two weeks before my delivery that Jonathan had gone to jail. I'm not sure why. He had been distant, but I figured it was because he had pressure from his coach, the basketball camp and our family had started sooner than we planned. My senior year was wrapping up and I missed prom, but I was happy to be able to attend graduation.

I was always known as the quiet girl who kept to herself. In fact, no one at school noticed that I was pregnant, nor believed I was pregnant. Mr. Frierson, the assistant principal, showed up at our home a few weeks before graduation. He assumed I had cancer and that was why I was on homebound. I told Mr. Frierson, "I didn't have cancer, I had a baby."

Mr. Frierson said, "Jones, you were one of the good girls, I didn't see that coming at all."

Daddy, holding the baby in his arms, immediately said, "She's still a good girl."

Mr. Frierson said, "Yes, Mr. Jones, I didn't mean she wasn't. Well, I'm glad you don't have cancer. I brought your cap and gown, and I wish you all the best."

When I showed up for graduation, everyone was so glad to see me. I learned while I was on homebound Mr. Frierson wasn't the only who assumed that I had cancer, and everyone was in disbelief I had a child.

My parents were really proud that I was graduating. They both stepped into the role of grandparent right after my son was born. After the ceremony, I wanted to show a few of my classmates, who thought I wasn't telling the truth, the baby. I had several classmates following me to see the baby, but my parents surprised me. They took him home with them, so I could have a good time out with my cousins Erica and Jan, who were visiting from Hawaii. We all geared up for a night of fun.

I had to admit, taking care of a baby was much more work than I'd anticipated. I was excited to have a free night off just to be a teenager, instead of a teenager with a baby. I was missing Jonathan and wishing he was there to celebrate with me. I could not wait for us to be together as a family.

When Jonathan returned home from jail after almost a year, he was just meeting our son. Jonathan told me over the phone he didn't want us to look at him through glass at the jail. I also found out that he wasn't being totally honest about the basketball camp. Jonathan had not been the same since his uncle passed away, and he lost all of his scholarships. He did attend the camp, but was asked to leave, due to not getting along with his coach and teammates. He'd been getting into fights almost every day.

Jonathan got his diploma while in jail. He still believed he was getting into college and going to play professional basketball. I believed in him, went to the park and watched him play basketball for hours. I liked watching him play, he was very passionate and dedicated and appeared to be back on track. Jonathan seemed the happiest while playing ball.

In the beginning, Jonathan spoke very well, definitely not like a kid from the projects. He even took a foreign language. Sometimes he would speak French to me. He would say, "Belle fille sera toujours à moi," which meant, "Beautiful girl will always be mine." Suddenly, he started speaking a lot of slang.

Jonathan knew my parents didn't want us together, but he had always been very respectful to them. He started coming by my parents' house really late. One night, Daddy walked up to where we were sitting in the car just talking.

Daddy knocked on the window. "Boy, what the hell are you doing at my house this late?"

Jonathan said, "I came to see my son."

"At two o'clock in the morning? Boy, you think I'm stupid? Where were you when this boy was being born? Did you bring some diapers and milk with you? You didn't!"

He called me into the house and told Jonathan he had to leave and didn't want him coming back around the house.

I knew Daddy was serious about not allowing Jonathan to come around. I felt that Daddy was being unfair and he was just upset because I wasn't his little girl anymore. I had to show him and Mama I could take responsibility and take care of my baby on my own.

I ran into Jonathan's cousin, Alberta. Alberta had three children now, and she had her own place. I asked how she could afford her own place and she told me how I could apply for an apartment, and they would go by my income at Burger King. She also told me how to apply for food stamps. I never knew anything about these things. I guess it made sense when Mama would say, "The government never gave me nothing, I took care of my children."

Unfortunately, I didn't have that same luxury, Jonathan and I weren't married, and I didn't have two incomes. Jonathan had a hard time finding a job, and he was more focused on pursuing his career in basketball, so he spent most of his time practicing.

After applying for the apartment, I had my own apartment within two months.

When I told my parents, Daddy was furious and he begged me to stay home, so I could concentrate on school. Mama didn't actually believe I was going to actually go through it. She said, "Jones, quiet down. That girl isn't going anywhere and if she does, she will be back."

I completely ignored them. I wanted to have a place that Jonathan could come to anytime he wanted. For a few months after moving in, I barely spoke to my parents. Daddy called, but most of the time, I let the answering machine pick up. Some mornings when I left for work, I would have a dozen roses outside my door, but there was never a card. I thought it was Daddy's way of saying that they were thinking about me. I guess I was being stubborn, because I never called to thank Daddy for the flowers. I missed my parents, but I was happy.

Jonathan came over as much as he wanted and a few months later, I found out I was pregnant again. I kept the faith, even though things weren't unfolding the way I planned, great things were still to come. We already had a boy and now, just maybe, it will be a girl. To my surprise, once again, Jonathan was arrested. I was not sure what he had done this time, and he continued with the tradition of not seeing his son and me, while in jail. He claimed he didn't want to expose me or our son to the prison environment.

Our son was getting big and no longer eating baby food, and with me being pregnant, I was eating more than what I got with food stamps. After arriving home from work one day, I looked over, and saw Daddy was in the parking lot. I opened the door and he came in behind me, carrying bags of groceries and household items.

I gave Daddy a big hug and thanked him for the groceries.

He said, "Baby girl, don't ever get too grown to talk to your mama and daddy. You never know how long we'll be here."

Daddy suddenly noticed I was pregnant again. "So, you about to be a mom again, Rhonda?"

"Yes, Daddy."

Daddy asked, "How are things working out?"

I wanted to tell him it was hard. Jonathan was in jail, my job at Burger King barely paid the bills, and I was tired of not having any furniture, but grateful the baby had a crib. Instead, I said things were going well and I had started classes at Midlands Technical College. Which technically was the truth, however, I dropped all my classes once I found out I was pregnant again.

Daddy picked up the flowers and he said, "Oh, the funny-looking boy got you some flowers?"

"No, Daddy, I know they're from you."

"No, baby girl, I didn't send any flowers. I was waiting on the right time to come by, and gave you some space."

I thought, if wasn't Daddy sending the flowers, then maybe it could be Jonathan. It was good to imagine Jonathan was getting back to being that thoughtful and loving young boy I'd met years ago.

After Daddy put the groceries in the kitchen, I immediately put the baby in his arms. He said, "This is a beautiful boy, even though he looks like that funny-looking boy."

"You're right, Daddy, because he looks nothing like me."

"So, where is the funny-looking fellow?"

"His name is Jonathan, Daddy, and he has freckles. What is so funny-looking about that? He will be coming home soon."

"Coming home from where, jail? I know you're not letting him stay here. That funny-looking boy can't even buy you any furniture. Got you sleeping and eating on the floor."

"Daddy, I got myself sleeping on the floor. This is my apartment and my responsibility."

"Look here, I know you moved out, so you can be with that trifling thug! Baby girl, you don't need anything from him or his people. Move back home where you belong. You can go away to college instead of that technical school."

"I'm not leaving my baby, Daddy, or Jonathan. Jonathan and I are going to be together. I know that's not what you want to hear, but trust me; I won't work at Burger King forever."

"You don't have to work right now, just move back in with us."

"No, Daddy, I cannot see myself doing that. I'm waiting to see what plans Jonathan has for us when he comes home. You never let Jonathan come to the house in the past. Will Jonathan be able to come to the house?"

"I love you, but no! I don't want that boy around my house. You can find someone else, but he isn't worth your time."

"Okay, Daddy, I understand but I'm going to have to pass. I'll just stay here and wait for Jonathan. It's going to be all right."

"Rhonda, listen, if you insist, he can come as far as the front porch, but that's it."

"Daddy, it's fine. I can stay here. You and Mama can have the house to yourselves."

"We want you home! Can't you see he is playing you? That boy is trash and a player."

"Okay, Daddy, whatever."

"You have changed so much. Do you love that boy more than your daddy? It's never been this hard to get you to listen."

"Daddy, I'm listening to you. I just don't agree with what you're saying."

"Rhonda, ever since you got hooked up with that boy, it's like you lost all your good senses. I'm asking you nicely. Come home and let us help you! You are a beautiful and smart young lady, and you deserve so much better. This boy isn't taking care of the children he already has."

"Children, Daddy? He only has one, and this one on the way, and he helps and much as he can. He is working hard to play college basketball and then he will get in the NBA."

"Rhonda, you cannot be this naïve, he is a drug dealer and a drug user, and he has a child older than this boy."

"Daddy, I'm not sure where you got your information, but that's not true. I had his first child."

"Not so. Your mama's friend, Cheryl, whose daughter works at the correctional center where that boy is doing his time, said he's been having visits and it hasn't been you and my grandson. He is seeing this woman and her son, and from what she told us, that boy is about four years old, his first son."

"Daddy, why are you saying this stuff? I'm not coming back home, no matter what you say."

"I have no reason to lie to you. It's true. That boy ain't what you thought and he can rot in jail for all I care, and stay the hell away from you and my grandson."

I got very quiet, I literally zoned out. I could see Daddy's mouth moving, but I couldn't tell you what he was saying anymore. I was so angry about what he was saying. But, I also realized Jonathan was all I thought about. I thought about how I could improve myself for him. Every one of my goals were built around him. Jonathan had actually become some type of god to me.

After standing there like an unresponsive statue, Daddy slapped me in the face.

Before I knew it, I was yelling at my daddy, something I never did before in my life. I yelled, "I hate you! Leave my house!" Immediately, I wanted to take back the words I said.

Daddy's eyes were fiery red and watery. He said, "I'm sorry I hit you. I didn't mean it. I love you and I just want you to wake up." He grabbed his hat and keys, and he left.

I was hurt and ashamed. I didn't know why I would say such a thing. I loved my dad, and I knew he loved me. I felt like I was the devil, and evil had gotten a tight grip on me.

About an hour later, Mama called. "You told your daddy you hate him? Honor thy mother and father, Rhonda, so your days will be long on the earth. You've really lost your mind, girl. You better drop to your knees and get your butt back in church before you go straight to hell."

I hung up with Mama and did just that, dropped to my knees. "Father, I sense that You are here watching me. Why are you so silent, or am I hard of hearing? Why am I being tortured by the desires that you said were my portion? You said I could have these things. I know I haven't done things the way You wanted me to, but I'm trying to make it right." I thought, *is going to church really going to solve all my problems*? "Lord, please answer as soon as possible. Amen."

Jonathan came home, and I didn't want to ruin our happy moments, so I didn't question him about what Daddy was saying. It was my twenty-first birthday, so we went out to celebrate. While in the club Jonathan got into it with this guy and a group of his friends. The guy claimed Jonathan owed him money. Before I knew it, beer bottles were smashed over Jonathan and his cousin's heads, then suddenly, shots were fired. I found myself under the table.

The police entered and everyone went running outside. I went searching for Jonathan and found him in the back of the police car. Jonathan's cousin, Darryl came up to me and told me Jonathan had drugs on him, and there was a warrant for his arrest. The last time Johnathan went to jail, the judge gave him probation. He violated it, so this time he was in prison for a few years.

After six months in prison, with me calling almost every day, Jonathan wrote me a letter and told me he was in love with someone else, but we could be friends. By this time, my parents' and my phone bill was over three thousand dollars. I remember sitting in the very dark, pitch black hallway of my parents' home, while reading his words over and over again. I sat in silence, hoping for a torch light to shine, to lead me to the next phase of my life. I felt the lover of my soul had abandoned me.

Emotional Murder

Chapter 8

SOUL TIES

Jonathan was sweet, gentle, charming, gifted, and handsome. He was everything that I ever longed for and probably even more. He made me smile, he made me laugh, and he made me feel good about myself. Each day he made me fall for him all over again. Suddenly, all the love songs started making sense. As much I tried, I couldn't let go of having a future with him, no matter how many times he rejected me.

Two years drifted by quickly. We had the boy and girl we talked about. I enrolled back at Midlands Technical College and was undecided about a major. I thought of becoming a school teacher. I wanted to be more than just a teacher, I wanted to be a protector because for some reason could spot a predator a mile away. I thought of being in the medical field like I had planned. With the help of Jonathan, I had gotten much better with math. Helping others people really made me feel good about myself. Being back in school gave me opportunity to be around more than just my parents and the children.

I met up with a few classmates from a study group. They tried to set me up with some of their guy friends.

They claimed I was too serious and needed to go out on a date. I will admit, I entertained the thought at times. Jonathan was my first and only boyfriend. I felt betrayed. I was only supposed to have sex with my husband. I always felt uneasy about being touched, but for some reason, I didn't feel uncomfortable with Jonathan. I was back to the point where I believed that kissing was completely gross, and sex was even grosser, especially if it wasn't Jonathan. Mama was happy I was going to church again. Even though, I felt like church was a chore and a tradition. I was back in the mode of saving myself for marriage, and now Mama and God will be much happier with me.nes

I was really gearing towards the medical field. I started harassing this couple at our church, who had their own private family practice. Their practice sponsored a certificate program for nursing assistants. I wasn't sure I wanted to be a nurse, but this would have been a good start to figure out where I fit in. Dr. and Mrs. Hayes agree to let me work at their practice on a trial basis.

I continued going to school at night. Dr. Hayes introduced me to Nurse Vivian, who'd been with the Hayes ever since they opened up their practice twenty years ago. Vivian was a registered nurse, and the nursing supervisor. Dr. Hayes stated Vivian would make a great mentor, and that she was just as knowledgeable as he was, if not more. He claimed he would ruin the practice without her. After hearing all the great things about Vivian, even from the other staff of nurses, I was honored and blessed that she wanted to mentor me. Mr. Hayes told me Vivian volunteered to mentor, as soon as she heard I was coming.

Vivian was intelligent, beautiful, confident and very passionate about nursing. I walked in the office on the first day. I didn't think I needed scrubs for training, my parents were already helping so much financially, so I didn't want to ask for money.

Vivian walked up and said, "What's your size?"

I told her size ten.

"Come to my office, I have some scrubs just your size."

She asked, "Hey, Dr. Hanyes told me you are in school, and that you are a mother of two children. I really commend you for continuing your education and maintaining your responsibility of being a mother."

"Yes, it can be overwhelming, but I am managing. I don't think I can handle anything else though."

Vivian was very nice, just as everyone had said, and she was also very patient. She taught me about the different medications, and I practiced taking her blood pressure. She even let me practice drawing her blood. Vivian said if I continued to do well, she would get the doctor to give me a scholarship so I wouldn't have to pay for nursing school. Vivian made nursing look effortless, she was so natural and her patients loved her. Vivian mentioned she thought about going back to school for a doctorate, but was looking to have more children. That was the first time I had heard Vivian speak on something personal concerning herself. Our conversations were always about medical equipment and patients. She made me think about my future.

Daddy was always trying to get me to come back home, but I was happy being on my own even though it was a struggle.

Jonathan had become distant with his calls and his presence. He never gave me a reason why he didn't call me for a week or come by to see the children. Weeks turned into months. He always used to come back, but he never gave me a reason for all those calls he ignored or all the times he hadn't been there. I knew I had become emotionally and spiritually bonded to him, but I refused to cut him off and set boundaries with him.

One day, there was a knock at the door. It was Jonathan. I stood there, and he let himself in inquiring, "Who's sending you flowers?"

"I don't know, they have been showing up for long time now. I thought maybe they were from you. Around this time, cassette tapes started to appear with the flowers. I had been so busy with the children, work and school, I didn't have time to listen, I started putting them in a shoebox under my bed.

"See, I know you're not the flowers type chick, you like books and journals, and what not. So, some nigger sending you flowers and tapes, and you don't know who it is? You expect me to believe that, you're not giving him what's mine?"

"No, I'm not!"

His light brown eyes were fiery red at this point. I noticed Jonathan was sporting a totally different look. His hair was braided back in cornrows, and he had facial hair. He was dressed in baggy jeans and a t-shirt. Jonathan was always very well dressed, and his clothes always fit perfectly. Trying not to give into my soulish desires, I ran to the bathroom to try to get myself together.

A few moments later, he knocked on the door. "What's wrong with you?"

I yelled back, "Nothing. Just give me a minute." I stood in the mirror having a "come to Jesus" meeting. I don't think Jesus did any talking. My hormones override his voice. Even though Jonathan had a new look, he was ruggedly handsome. I said to myself, "Come on, Rhonda. Get it together. Go out there and stand your ground. Ask him why he's here, and then ask him to leave." I walked out of the bathroom feeling bold and confident.

Before I asked the question, he said, "I came to see the kids."

"Why do you want to see them now? You didn't want to see them when you were locked up or at least that's what you told me. You can just stay across town, living with your other woman and her kid."

"First of all, that is my oldest son's mama. We not together, we just good friends. Your daddy and moms don't like me anyway, so I felt like it was best to push you away. I didn't want to deal with the drama."

"It's funny you would use that as an excuse, because I moved out of their house, so you could feel comfortable being with your son and me."

"Don't be mad. I love you."

"Don't be mad? Really? I'm not mad. I'm hurt that you didn't even have the decency to tell me face-to-face that you have another child and that you are in love with some other chick. It has taken me some time, but I'm putting myself back together with the strength of the Lord and help from my parents. So, you can leave and go back wherever you came from. I am so over the back and forth with you."

"I thought about you the whole time I was locked up. Out of all the ladies I have been with, you are the hardest to deal with."

I just looked. Not only did he look different, but his game was also off.

"What I mean is you made me nervous. I was thinking that I wasn't good enough, and that your parents were right. I didn't deserve to be with you. You were raised differently than me, and I didn't know if I could live up to your expectations. I need my basketball career to maintain a relationship with somebody like you. You look so beautiful and I want you so bad. Sometimes I wondered if that made me selfish. I realized that other girl was just something to do. I didn't have to try hard with them."

I thought, *Reject him. Don't fall for this!*

We sat on the couch face-to-face, and I was looking into his eyes. He seemed sincere. He kissed me on my neck, and I blacked out, not literally, but into his trance. Unfortunately, I got tangled up, and my soul joined with him once again.

I didn't want to tell my parents Jonathan was coming back around again. So, the children were back in daycare. My parents hated the children going to daycare, but it kept them from being at my apartment so often. On weekends, I would catch the bus, and drop the children off. I tried to convince them having the children in daycare would increase their socialization skills, and it was like being in school which help them stay ahead. I'm almost certain Mama didn't believe I was being completely truthful, but she didn't say anything.

Jonathan promised he was looking for a job. I prayed he would find something soon.

I was getting the children dressed and Jonathan was still sleep in the bed when there was a knock at the door. It was the police with a warrant to arrest Jonathan for nonpayment of child support. I knew it wasn't his oldest son's mother because even though she allowed Jonathan to see his son, her current husband adopted her son, so he wasn't obligated to pay child support. After Jonathan left with the police

The phone rang, and there was a female on the other end saying, "Have they picked him yet? Yeah, I knew he would be over there with your pitiful self. Go ahead and pay that money for your man, so I can have my money for bike week."

Jonathan fathered another child, child number four.

I didn't know what to believe at this point. I was in such a dark place. I became a predator, murdering my own destiny. I didn't understand why I continued to allow this chaos in my life and called it love. I turned on the stereo Anita Baker's "No More Tears."

"And there's no more tears
And no more saddened eyes
From crying through the night
Gonna gather up, gather up my feelings
And lock them all inside."

That was exactly what I was going to do. I was going to stop all that crying and lock up my feelings. My feelings were holding me hostage, and I hadn't been able to complete any of my goals.

Chapter 9

MYSTERIOUS DELIVERIES

The flowers and tapes continued to mysteriously appear on my front door. One evening my next-door neighbor, Janey, a middle-aged lady, stood at her door and said, "Pretty flowers. I saw that handsome, mocha brown, young brother putting those flowers at your door."

"Okay. Wow! Ms. Janey, so you actually have seen the person leaving the flowers."

Janey said, "Yes honey. I know one thing it wasn't that funny-looking dude with the freckles everywhere. I tell you that. He's cute and all, but he nothing like this one. You got it going on, girl."

"Ms. Janey, I have no clue who the man is leaving flowers and tapes."

"Well, if you don't want to know him, I will get to know him."

"Ms. Janey, you a mess."

"Yes, girl, I will mess his head right on up since you don't want him."

It was really starting to get weird that this guy had never shown himself. I had a few minutes before the daycare van dropped off the children and took out a few cassette tapes from the shoe box. I popped in the first tape, the music was louder than his words. He was saying my name over and over. Until you come back to me…" Luther Vandross played in the background. The man talked about how much he loved me and the children and that we'll be together soon. I was no longer flattered, instead, I felt unnerved, his voice sounded kind of creepy.

My cousin Erica was in town, she talked me into going out, and she volunteered to watch the children. I went to the Fountain Blue with some of my classmates and the Fresh Prince and DJ Jazzy Jeff made an appearance at the club. We were on the dance floor all night, before I knew it after three o'clock in the morning.

As soon as I turned the key, Erica was out the door and in her car. It seemed as soon as I laid down in the bed, the alarm clock went off. It was 4:30 a.m. and I only had a few minutes to get the kids dressed and to catch the 5:45 a.m. bus. Erica had already put the kids' clothes out and packed their bags. I took a quick shower, changed my underwear, slipped on my scrubs, dressed the kids, and we are out the door at 5:15 a.m. I swung the door open and saw a shadow coming up behind me. It was still a bit dark. I heard a voice say, "Hello, beautiful." I slowly turned around, and it was a tall, mocha-colored man with brown eyes standing behind me.

He said, "Remember me?"

"No, sorry. I don't. I'm trying to get to the bus stop."

"I can take you to work."

"Thanks. That's all right. We're fine."

"I'm not a stranger. You can ride with me. I'm Fred, and I used to sit behind you in middle school. We worked together at Burger King for about three weeks."

I didn't want to appear rude, but I didn't remember him at all.

"Oh, Fred. Okay. Good seeing you."

I finished locking the door and walked away with the kids.

Fred followed. "I want to take you out. I want to be with you."

"Fred, I'm sorry. I have a boyfriend."

"No, you don't. You have a dude who fathered your children. He doesn't love you. I do. I give you flowers, and I make music for you. He doesn't even take care of his kids, and he keeps making more."

Fred was being very polite, yet I still was a little fearful, and didn't want to upset him.

"Fred, I don't want to be rude, but I'm not about to discuss this with you. I have to catch the bus."

He grabbed my arm, and he looked very agitated. His face was very sweaty. "I love you."

My heart dropped down, I almost dropped the children backpacks. "You don't even know me."

"I know you. I know your favorite color used to be yellow, but you wear a lot of black now when you're not in your scrubs. You used to love bright colors, but your colors have changed to dark ones. He is changing you, he's making you dark. I know you like writing, which you rarely do anymore. I know you're very quiet and shy especially around people you don't know. I know you love God, but you get confused a lot, wondering if you could really please God."

I was shocked, confused, and scared all at the same time. Fred kept talking. "Beautiful, I have been praying that you would leave that sorry dude alone for a while now." Fred came very close like he wanted to kiss me.

I went around his arm hanging against the door.

"Fred, it was nice meeting you, but I'm about to miss my bus and be late for work."

"I can take you to work. I'm meant to take care of you."

I had my backpack on my back and both kids on my hip. I ran down the street to the bus stop.

He came behind me. The bus was already at the stop, and I got on with the kids.

My head was spinning, and my heart was racing. I had no clue how that dude knew so much of my business.

I started to think back to when I first moved into the apartment, and it felt like someone was there.

It was that sensation you get when you can just feel someone watching you. I heard things outside of the window in the kitchen. I would up and looked around the kitchen and dining area and through the windows, but I didn't see anything. I still felt eyes on me. The phone would ring in the middle of the night and but it was a wrong number, I brushed it off. I blamed it on nerves and the fear of being alone in my own place for the first time. Now I wondered if it had been Fred the whole time.

It was quite an unusual morning.

I got off the first bus and dropped the kids off at the daycare. I walked down to catch the next bus to get to work. I noticed Fred tailing me. I turned around to confront him, asking, "What? What do you want?"

He laughed and shouted back, "You, beautiful!" He kept following me. It became weird and scary.

"I'm calling the police!" I ducked into a corner store, and he didn't follow me in. He stood on the outside.

"I will be back for you. You are mine. I don't want to harm you. I want to take care of you."

A guy in the store said, "Hey, is that dude bothering you?"

"Yes, sir, he is."

The guy went out, and Fred walked down the street as if he wasn't just yelling in the store. The guy came back inside the store. "He's gone now."

I finally made it to work. Vivian let me know she was not pleased with me showing up to work late. Not looking up from the desk, she commanded, "Rhonda, go ahead and get the blood work from Mr. DeWright. She said, "Why in the world are you sweating like that? You know what, I don't want to know."

Vivian knew some of the history between Jonathan and me, and she never gave her opinion, she would just listen.

I knew I was up late and I ran to the bus, but I was still gasping for my breath. I was also feeling very fatigued. I didn't want to disappoint Vivian, so going back home wasn't an option. I went inside the exam room and greeted Mr. DeWright.

Mr. DeWright was a patient who had been coming to the office for years. He came in a few months ago complaining of cold sweats, weight loss, loose stools, and unexplained sores on his skin. I never asked anyone about their personal business, mainly because I didn't want people asking me about my business, and I respect people's privacy. I did make sure the patients felt comfortable. I made goody bags, so they would be more comfortable while they wait. I kept water stocked as well. I would check on them and offer them water. Very often, the patients shared thoughts and feelings that they wouldn't normally share, telling me about things that most people keep private.

Mr. DeWright was the pastor of a well-known ministry. Most of the staff in the office called him, the seer, another name for a prophet. There was no essential difference between a seer, "one who sees prophetic visions" and a prophet or "one who is called by God to be His spokesperson." I believe Mr. DeWright was both.

I heard he warned Vivian that her first husband was planning on leaving her and that he was going to get full custody of their three children. He encouraged her to spend more time with her husband and children.

Vivian said she always thought Mr. DeWright was too religious, and she did not pay him any mind." She said, "Mr. DeWright needs to see about his own sins, before I take anything he said seriously." Vivian worked at the hospital as well, and she worked twenty hours most days. One morning, her husband got up for work, dressed the children for school, and told Vivian he needed her signature on some papers for a new bank account he just opened for his new business. Vivian realized the next day that she had signed divorce papers, also giving her husband full custody of the children. She returned to an empty house that evening.

When she checked the voicemail, her husband left her a message saying that he started a law firm in New Mexico and was getting married again in three weeks. According to Vivian, she did not see it as a warning, but believed that Mr. DeWright had cursed her.

I didn't know anything about prophets of today. I grew up in a nice conservative Baptist ministry, but I didn't believe Mr. DeWright had cursed her. He was far from perfect, but we are dealing with something.

One day, while I was getting Mr. DeWright's vitals, he grabbed my hand and said, "You are not crazy. You see things, and you know things about people. That is the Holy Spirit speaking to you. I see you walking fast through pouring rain holding an umbrella. I hear the Holy Spirit saying it's a new season, put the umbrella aside and continue forward. I see the cloudy gray skies turn bright blue and beautiful sunshine. I see you look up with a big smile, receiving glory from the Lord and feeling warm sunshine on your face. I hear the Holy Spirit saying you are faithful, determined, strong, focused, but tender and compassionate and so very wise for your age. It's the knowledge and understanding that the Holy Spirit has placed inside you. You have to give yourself completely over to him. Go forward with confidence and boldness as he has already equipped you and qualified you with whatever you could possibly need.

"The Holy Spirit will set you up and bring sweet wounded people your way for you to minister to through your life's truths, and you will encourage them and comfort them with the same comfort God has comforted you with. It flows out of you. You will bring others to repentance and set them free to pursue God and fall in love with Him. I see you ministering to everyone but especially women of all ages because of the tenderness in your heart. You look at people with very little judgement, but you see it as a sign of weakness. But, it's actually your strength. The Lord will use you mightily, young lady. You shall prophesy to regions and beyond. That is the word of the Lord concerning you."

I did not know how to respond to what he said, so I just looked at him and smiled. I felt overwhelmed because it felt like a huge responsibility. But I already had a lot of responsibilities. I did not have much knowledge about prophesying. I wasn't too sure about everything he was saying, but I took notice of the fact that when he started to open up to me about his personal life, it was like he was not telling me anything new. It was as though I already knew everything he was saying.

Mr. DeWright was married with four children, but he explained that he often had extramarital affairs with men. He believed that love was not gender-specific, and we should have the right to love men and women as attraction allowed.

After several tests, we confirmed that he had contracted the Human Immunodeficiency Virus, also known as HIV. He was in denial about his diagnosis and went several months without treatment. This particular day, he came in because he had passed out Sunday morning, right before he got ready to preach. He lost a significant amount of weight, and he had skin rashes all over his body. He was visibly ill. After reviewing his lab work, the doctor determined that his CD4 count was very low, and his HIV had progressed. I lifted his arm, and one of his sores was leaking green and yellow pus. I became nauseated, the room was spinning, and sweat was pouring off my body, I passed out in front of him.

Vivian rushed over to collect the blood from Mr. DeWright so that his blood did not squirt out all over the office. The other office staff rushed over to assist me.

I was only out a few seconds. Linda, one of the nurses who worked in the office, wiped the sweat from my face. I tried to run to the trash can. I held my mouth, but I couldn't stop it. I threw up all over the office. I tried to get to the bathroom and it continued to come up. I finally made it to the bathroom. I was completely embarrassed. I lay on the bathroom floor, feeling like I had been run over by a bus several times.

Vivian knocked on the door, and then she came in with clean scrubs and a urine cup in her hand. She said, "Get changed and pee in this cup."

"Why would I pee in the cup? Are you trying to do a drug test on me? You know I don't do drugs."

"I know you not doing drugs, but you're having sex with that baby making, drug selling, drug addict."

"Why are you talking about Jonathan like that? I thought you liked him."

"Girl, please. I tolerate him, but I never said I like him."

"Listen, Vivian. I appreciate everything you have done for me, but I won't trash talk Jonathan, nor allowed anybody else to do it."

"Can't you see what he's doing? He's bringing you down with him. Get a clue, girl, before you go completely dark and never turn back."

Vivian told me she would close the office alone, and that I should go home. She warned me to make sure I arrived on time tomorrow. I begged her not to tell the Hayes what happened, I didn't want them looking at me differently, especially after they gave me a chance to prove myself, and had already agreed to sponsor my career, even if I wanted to go straight for my MD.

That night, as I washed my face getting ready for bed, I thought maybe I should have taken the pregnancy test. I couldn't be pregnant because there was no way I could handle another child. Things were already so out of order. Jonathan and I couldn't be more distant. Yet, I continued to sleep with him whenever he dropped by, convincing myself it really wasn't sinning because he was my husband already in my heart. Jonathan had some things he needed to work through and so did I.

There was a Revco Pharmacy a few blocks away from my apartment. I decided to pick up a pregnancy test, so I walked and meditated. I was completely exhausted when I returned home. I opened the test and peed on the stick and lay across the bed for a few minutes. The next morning, I woke up to the plus sign. I hadn't seen Jonathan for a few weeks now; he was on his usual hiatus. I didn't concern myself with his absence. All I could think about was how I didn't want to have another child.

I arrived at work on time, yet feeling very tired. I was in the midst of pouring a cup of coffee when Vivian walked in.

"You shouldn't be drinking coffee. It's not good for the baby."

I looked up thinking, *Okay, now she is a prophet*?

She said, "I've known for several weeks now. You've gained a little weight just around your stomach area. Normally you barely eat lunch, but for the last few weeks, you've been sending for lunch along with everyone else. I'm not trying to get in your business, but what are you going to do?"

"Vivian, I'm not keeping it."

"Rhonda, think about your options. It's important to take the time to make the decision that's right for you, but it's also important to make that decision as soon as possible. Abortion is safe, but like all medical procedures, there are risks. The chance of those risks occurring increases the longer you're pregnant.

"It's simple, I have made the decision, I cannot care for another child, nor is it fair to ask my parents for help. I am not having this child."

"Rhonda, you don't have to worry, I could be the baby's godmother. You wouldn't have to worry about anything. I would babysit."

"Vivian, you not getting it, I am still on my parents' medical insurance. I am not going through this. I have too much going right now, and I barely have time for the children I already have."

"Okay, Rhonda, I have an even better idea. You can have the child and give it to me."

"Vivian, are you serious! I really can't talk about this right now."

I realize as days went by, Vivian was really serious about me having the baby and giving it to her. Every morning, Vivian brought me breakfast. The embryo inside of me was always hungry, which didn't help me resist the yellow grits and cheese, liver pudding, onion sausage, turkey bacon, and ginger ale with green tea to wash it all down. Each week, Vivian was even more persistent.

As I indulged in what I believed to be a heaven-sent meal, Vivian had gone back to her office. I looked up and a giant, middle-aged man was standing in the doorway. My eyes were immediately drawn in the direction of a man who was six feet seven and maybe taller. He had a muscular build, not overly muscular, jet black hair, dark brown eyes, and a strong jaw. Darwin Williams was a lawyer, a minister at one of the mega churches here in town. Darwin and Vivian were engaged to be married. I heard one of the nurses say that Vivian vowed never to get married again, unless she could have the full package again; career, husband and children.

Darwin said, "Hello, that food smells good, did you save some for me?"

"Hey Mr. Williams, no, I just finished it all, sorry. I will go get Vivian for you."

Darwin said, "I'm here to see you. Vivian speaks very highly of you. She said you're very knowledgeable about the patients' needs even before any tests are done on them. I told her that's the Holy Spirit working in that girl. Yeah, you know being a nurse isn't your only calling."

"Yes, sir, I think of being a doctor or a teacher."

"No, I am saying you got a call on your life to preach the gospel."

"Oh wow, you like the second person to say that to me. I love God, and I love helping people, but I don't see me being in any pulpit anytime soon."

"See, you don't have to tell me. I see the glow of the Lord all over you. Listen, Vivian told me about your situation, and there's nothing to be ashamed of. We all fall short and sin sometimes. I know that being a single mother of two and having another child would be overwhelming for you. Children are a blessing from God, and it's serious when we don't obey God."

"It was good to see you, Mr. Williams, but I have to get to work now."

"Wait. I have something for you."

Darwin handed me papers, a contract agreement to give Vivian and him custody of my baby. He said a different contact would be drawn up once I actually have the baby.

He also handed me an envelope. I looked in the envelope, and there was a check for forty thousand dollars in it.

I was shocked, and this point. I didn't know what to think.

Mr. Williams said, "You don't have to worry about catching the bus." He handed me a key.

"This is a joke, right?" I walked out to the parking garage, and there was a brand-new 1993 Toyota Camry. I said, "I don't even know how to drive yet."

"You're twenty-two years old and don't know how to drive?"

"No, I don't. Neither do my mother or my oldest sister, who is thirty something."

"I tell you what. I will teach you. I will come by on the weekends early in the mornings."

I started to think maybe this would be a blessing for all us. "I'm really tired of dragging the children on the bus, and I wouldn't have to get up so early. Let me think about it."

"I believe God sent me to you to help you make the right decision. If you have the abortion, you will be a murderer. If you give the baby to Vivian and me, you'll save your soul, and you can provide a better life for your other children."

"I still have time, and I need to think about it."

Darwin drove me home in the car.

I started to really consider giving them the baby, they both were really good people, and would provide the child with so much.

Darwin started taking me out early Saturday and Sunday morning. We started out driving on country roads. Two weeks had gone by and I was getting better, but not ready to drive on the highway. I had trouble with three-point turns. I was on spring break at school. Vivian said I could have the week off with pay, so I could focus on preparing for the driving test. Darwin was outside my apartment waiting for me. I was really nervous because we were going to drive on the highway today.

"I can tell you're anxious. Just relax. You're doing so well."

He was very patient, and I was very grateful that he was taking this time out of his busy schedule to help me. As we got on the highway, Darwin reached over and started rubbing my inner thigh. I swerved and almost ran into someone.

"Please don't do that."

"I'm just trying to relax you, baby."

I pulled over with my heart was racing. I was too nervous to drive back, so I allowed Darwin to drive. "I'm not relaxed. Let's just go back to my house, so you can drop me off."

I got out of the car, slamming the door.

He followed me to my door, kissing my neck as I tried to get my key out to open the door. I finally got the door open and was able to get in and push Darwin back, so he couldn't get inside. I stood on the other side of the door, wondering why every good thing that came by was always mixed with something very bad. It felt like I'd given everything I had. Was it too much to ask for pure love, love that doesn't want to use me or abuse me?

I prayed, "God, I want to serve you. I want to believe that You love me too, but it's hard. How can you be so silent in all of this? It's like I get out of a storm in my life, but not quite out of the storm, because it's still drizzling, with thunder roaring here and there. So, it leaves me unsure and confused. I walked around feeling cautious and numb. I continue to bury stuff. Then the next storm comes and I find myself walking around dazed and empty, feeling just enough to take care of these children."

I made some warm tea, and starting a hot bath, I heard loud knocking at the door. It was Vivian. She let herself in. "Darwin told me you had a bad day and refused to go back."

"Vivian, I was going to call."

"Call to tell me you decided to let us adopt the baby?"

I handed her the check and said, "I need some time off."

"So, you're going to kill this baby instead of giving it to me?"

She looked at me with fire flaming in her eyes. She said softly but firmly, "You will never forget this."

I apologized. "I can't go through this pregnancy. Please don't take it personally. I would love to help you if I could."

"You know you a piece of work, little girl. Up to this point, I always admired you for being strong, but you're weak. You're a weak little girl trying to be a woman. Real women take responsibility and make smart decisions."

"I'm taking responsibility, and I'm doing what's best for me."

"The problem is that you are a selfish, spoiled, weak, little girl, who is about to get a taste of this evil world. There will be hell to pay if you go through with this abortion! You will never be the same! You will hear babies crying for the rest of your life! You will be a murderer!"

As tears rolled down Vivian's face, I could tell she was very broken about this. I didn't understand why she didn't work this hard to keep her own biological children. I had never seen her this angry. I felt bad for her, but I was certain I wasn't having this child for her or anyone else. I couldn't believe she was speaking such spiteful words over my life. Her words burned in my soul, for that moment the guilt only lasted a few seconds. The guilt leaked out of my body.

I thanked her for her input, and I walked away feeling justified. With no facial expression, I asked her to leave my house.

Chapter 10

EMOTIONAL FREEDOM

My circumstances had changed my character. I was no longer the bright, bubbly person I used to be. I once used to speak my mind, now my mind speaks to me. I was constantly filled with paranoia, second guessing myself, and I cared way too much about what others thought of me. I wanted to reclaim my happiness. I would often walk around like a deer in headlights, blank, and empty as my soul searched for the answers it needed to cultivate positive emotions and transform the negative emotions of others into compassion. I wanted emotional freedom.

Somehow, Fred knew that I was pregnant again. One morning, I was getting ready to head to work. I was locking up the house, when I noticed the prettiest pink and red flowers sitting beside the door. Inside it was a card that read, "Do not have any more babies from that loser!" I knew it was Fred who had left the flowers. The extreme shock of emotions that entered my body caused me to drop the vase. Glass and flowers shattered everywhere. I was terrified that Fred was continuing to monitor my every move. However, he seemed to be pretty harmless as he had never tried to physical harm me. Mentally, I was terrified of what he may be capable of or potentially plotting behind the scene. It was a reason why he was monitoring my every move. I have no idea of what that reason could be.

Fred seemed to want what was best for me. He was good at offering unselecting advice through his recording and letters. I have no idea why I continued to entertain Fred in this manner, but I guess, maybe part of me knew he was right. Maybe part of me wished that Jonathan had paid the same amount of attention to me that Fred was. Maybe part of me wished that Jonathan was Fred. Fred would spend hours through his tape recordings telling me how I should stop partying so much, how I should dress, and how I should raise my children.

That Fred had some nerve.

Later on, that night, I had the worst time falling asleep. I laid awake, counting sheep. I tried drinking warm milk but that didn't help, just gave me an upset stomach. I tried reading my Bible, but that did not work either. Every time I would read something, my mind would drift off to something else and I could not focus. The time was around 3:00 a.m. and I could hear rumbling outside my home. I was startled, so I gathered my robe and a flashlight and went to sleep on the couch. Next thing I know I heard, *Bam*! *Bam*! *Bam*! on my front door.

"Rhonda, open up the door!"

I had not seen or heard from Jonathan in weeks. His eyes were fiery red and he had this awful body odor as if he had been sweating in a factory for days. Because I still had a soft heart for Jonathan, I invited him inside.

Jonathan replied, "Na...I'mma stay outside." He continues to tell me, "My life is hell right now. I tried to get away, I tried praying to this God, but nothing is working out for me."

I tried to understand what Jonathan was saying but he kept talking in codes or riddles and it was very hard to comprehend what he was trying to tell me. As I got closer to Jonathan, I tried to comfort him and calm him down.

He was startled and grew more enraged. Suddenly, Jonathan pulled a Glock out of his backside and pointed it to his head. He started shouting, "I am about to end this!"

By this point, I'm pleading with Jonathan to put the gun away, but he continued to make senseless talk. I told him how much I loved him. This made things worse because now, I was on the other side of the gun.

Jonathan explained, "You shouldn't love me. I am undeserving of love." He continued to provide this explanation of how he had gotten into some "heavy stuff" and that I could not handle the stuff he has gotten himself into. Jonathan then started going down this path of guilt tripping, insinuating that because I had my mom and dad, my life was better than his.

I asked, "Jonathan, where is this coming from? Why are you being this way?"

After many guilt trips and death threats, Jonathan explained that his uncle died. "He was the only father I ever knew, Rhonda! He motivated me to be great. He promised me he would be sitting in the stands at every game when I made it to the NBA."

Although I was still shaken up over the events that had just transpired with Jonathan pulling his gun on me, I tried to comfort him the best way I knew how without becoming his target. "Jonathan, your uncle is watching over you from heaven. His spirit will continue to live in your heart."

Jonathan slowly raised his head and looked up towards me as if he wanted to believe that what I was saying is true. He quickly turned the gun back on himself. The sob story was never-ending! After explaining about his uncle passing away, his grievances turned to his struggle of owing thousands in back child support.

At this point, I was drained. I had no more support to offer Jonathan and I really just wanted to get out of his way. If he was going to kill himself, I did not want to witness his death. I had children to care for and I was not ready to die. I told Jonathan it was best that he goes home and get some rest. We can finish discussing this when he felt better. I slowly opened the door and backed inside. Soon after, I heard this loud thumping noise. I rushed to the window to see what was going on. Jonathan had slammed the door to his car and was pulling out of the driveway.

The next morning, thoughts of Jonathan occupied my head space. Earlier, I learned from Jonathan's cousin, Kenely, that he had gotten expelled from school. Jonathan failed several tests, was accused of breaking and entering property and drawing graffiti on school buildings. With the thousands he owed in back child support and the passing of his uncle, I knew he could not handle the news of me being pregnant. If I would have told him, he probably would have killed me and the baby right then! Jonathan and I were not married, but I felt guilty for keeping this secret from him. Darwin and Vivian were the only ones who knew that I was pregnant and I felt like if I didn't tell Jonathan soon, then word would get out around town and he would eventually know that I was expecting.

Darwin and Vivian were very disappointed in me for getting pregnant by Jonathan again. Vivian appeared to be a conservative, well put together woman of class who conducted herself with extreme professionalism. Lately when I entered her presence, she would give off "angry black woman" vibes. She'd roll her eyes at me and look me up and down in disgust every time I entered the building.

It was cool and rainy outside. I was twenty weeks, just a few days from it being too late to have an abortion. I hadn't changed my mind. I wasn't keeping this baby. Daddy finally retired, and he bought his 1994 Cadillac just as he planned. He gave me his old Cadillac. While we stood in the yard, he handed me the keys and said, "Baby girl, I'm so proud of you. I'll always be here for you." My daddy's heart never lacked the passion a father feels for his daughter. He was always very present in my life. So, why was it that I didn't require that same passion and love from the man who was destined to be my husband? Why can't Jonathan love me that way? Why doesn't he care enough to come after me, make me feel safe, and wanted?

I lay in the back seat of the car while my cousin drove, and Rosa sat on the passenger's side. She asked, "Rhonda, are you okay?"

"Yes, Rosa. You've asked me that a million times already."

I asked my cousin, Gerald, to drive me because I knew he would agree without asking a bunch of questions. I hadn't seen Gerald in almost two years. Just as I thought, he agreed. I suppose he asked Rosa to come along in case I needed help with girl stuff. We drove about fifty miles. I enjoyed the complete silence.

Rosa said, "Have you spoken to Jonathan? What does he have to say? This really doesn't seem like anything you would do. You've always had such a big heart when it comes to children."

"So, my heart is bad towards children now that I am doing this?"

"I'm not saying that. You just seem different."

"Look, Rosa. I haven't heard from him in weeks. This is my body. I don't need his permission. I prefer not to talk about this. Can we ride in silence please? Gerald, I have an MP3 player and some earphones in the glove compartment if you really need music."

"Okay, I won't say anything else. But you know there are some fancy apartments beside ours. You can move over there, and that way we can carpool. You can have more support while you work and go to school."

I never used curse words because Mama Jones said only street women use curse words. I guess I was feeling really street right now. I was screaming on the inside, "Shut the hell up!" On the outside my body lay still in the back seat, allowing the vibration of Rosa's voice to be removed from my thoughts. At this point, I didn't even bother to formulate words. I closed my eyes and took myself to another place. I had this unusual craving for watermelon. I could see the nourishing, juicy, fresh fruit in my mind. I believed it would provide refreshment to everything in me.

Rosa got the clue from my body language and remained silent the rest of ride.

In the waiting room, there was dead silence. I scanned the room, and I noticed really young faces and a few that looked middle age.

I knew a few girls who had abortions. I couldn't believe I was here. Through church, I believed that abortion was murder. I felt I had already disappointed God by having sex before marriage, so what's one more thing on the list? Because of my beliefs, for a split second, I considered carrying the pregnancy to term. Nevertheless, I was not financially independent or secure, and I wasn't in a stable or even clearly defined relationship. I had goals that I wanted to accomplish that required a large degree of flexibility in my life. I had no intention of becoming pregnant, but unfortunately, I wasn't being smart. I was secretly annoyed by the ultrasound. I not only heard the heartbeat, but I could also see it. I felt if there was some part of me that actually wanted this child; it would mean that I hadn't become completely dark and heartless.

After the ultrasound, they sent me to do preliminary counseling. I went into a room, a huge office, with a couch and a chair in front of the desk. A lady sitting at the desk asked me questions. I sat straight up in my chair, smiling each time I spoke. I felt very on edge, very emotional, but I was clever enough to show no emotions. I didn't want them to refuse to do the procedure.

She discussed with me the risks of the abortion. I pretended to listen attentively. I signed some papers. I didn't even read them. I was then sent to make my payment. After they took my three hundred and sixty dollars, I went to take my pre-procedure medicine.

Because I was further along than most people having an abortion, I was actually put in pre-labor. Just three minutes later, I started to have monster cramps in my stomach. I had a pain that nearly knocked the wind out of me. Once I caught my breath, I knew immediately I had to stay focused and not feel. They gave me anesthesia to numb my bottom. I could have paid a hundred dollars more, and they would have put me to sleep. I was conscious the whole time. I felt slight discomfort, but it really wasn't anything worse than an extended pap smear.

I heard the low hum of the machine. I closed my eyes, and all I saw was black. The sound of the machine faded. The nurse rubbed my head and said I was doing well. Her voice faded, and I no longer felt her touch. I didn't hear anything or feel anything. I was numb emotionally and physically.

I only had minor cramps and moderate back pain over the weekend. The doctor said I could return to work on Monday.

Vivian was usually in her office, but this morning she wasn't there.

While I was getting supplies ready for the day, I started to have minor cramps and moderate back pain. As the morning continued, the cramps got stronger, and I felt something flowing. I went to the bathroom, and my scrubs were covered in blood. I went into the doctor's office, and I explained that I needed to go home.

The doctor said, "Vivian told us about your abortion. Of course, go ahead and go home and take it easy."

I walked out of the office, and all the nurses standing around the nurses' station looked at me. One of the nurses, Tammy, said, "Girl, don't be embarrassed. I've had five already."

I just looked and smiled. I felt completely betrayed. It was obvious Vivian had told everyone in the office about my abortion.

When I got home, I called Mama and asked if the children could stay with her and Daddy for a few days. I told her I had midterms coming up, and I had more duties at work. Mama agreed. She and Daddy were the perfect grandparents; they loved having the children at their house. Sometimes I thought the children loved being at my parents' house more than they liked being with me.

The bleeding got lighter, but my back was hurting so bad. The stomach cramps were monstrous. Every time I thought of Vivian telling everyone what I had done, my head started to hurt. The doctor at the clinic prescribed me some Motrin 800. I was only supposed to take two as needed. I took three. About thirty minutes later, I still had cramps, and my head was throbbing. I suddenly became really drowsy.

I dropped down on the couch. My mouth was dry. I was too weak to get back up. I turned off the lamp next to me, so the room was completely dark. As soon as I closed my eyes, there was a light knock at the door. I ignored it. Maybe I was dreaming. I opened my eyes, and I saw the knob turning. I yelled, "Who is it?"

I didn't hear anything, so I closed my eyes again.

Suddenly, I felt this wetness on my face. I was being kissed. He took off his shirt, and he unbuttoned mine. I tried to stand, but I was pushed back to the couch. He took off his pants.

I said, "I can't do this. I'm not well."

My heart was racing, and my body shook.

"He said, "This is going to make you feel better, beautiful."

I was wearing a shirt; he lifted me up and pulled the shirt off and took my bra off.

I said, "I can't have sex. Please, don't do this."

He put his hands inside my underwear.

I said "No, stop. I have my period."

I tried to move his hands away. He was on top of me and put his arms around me, so it was difficult for me to stop him. I tried to push my body upward and twist to move him, but he was so strong. I shouted, "Get off of me!" over and over.

Suddenly, he placed himself inside me, and we were having sex. I couldn't escape. I climaxed even though in my mind I didn't want to. I became paralyzed as he continued. He moaned and groaned and finally finished. Before removing himself from me, he kissed me on the forehead and said he loved me. He got dressed and left.

I tried to move. I wanted to believe that I was dreaming. My body was in pain, and I felt fatigued. I got up. It felt like I was spinning. I felt completely disgusted. I wanted to believe it was all a dream, but when he opened the door, the cold air woke me up a bit. I knew it was real. I said to myself, "I continue to do bad things, and bad things happen. Was this a bad thing? Am I being melodramatic?" I didn't scream. I didn't hit him. He was forceful, but not violent.

I made it to the door to lock it, and I fell to the floor. I turned on the light. I saw a trail of blood from the couch across the living room. I lay on the floor in excruciating pain, and my feelings dripped everywhere. My heart was bleeding, feeling like a sword was plunged right through it. I was slipping down into a pool of unwanted emotions.

Oh my God, the baby. I can't stop the baby from crying. I began self-medicating on anything I could get my hands on: alcohol, prescription pills, and even cutting myself to get relief. I became addicted to the night life, partying four to five nights a week and chasing a distraction that would get my mind off of anything that kept me in bondage to the things that happened to me.

I grew up in church, so I knew that God was not pleased with my behavior. They say that God forgives, but I was so far from God, it seemed impossible to even speak or hear from Him at the time. I was at the point where I was numb to life. I operated as a robot, completing activities and responding routinely. I awakened every morning at 6:20 a.m. to get the kids ready for school. I had my morning cocktail around 7:15 a.m., took a nap from 7:40 to 12:05 p.m. Then, I had an evening cocktail and a small bite to eat, just enough to sober up before the kids came home from school. I put on my best tilted smile and greeted each of them with a hug.

"How was school today?" The white noise that constantly played in my brain made it difficult to hear their responses.

After the kids were settled in with my parents, I mustered up enough strength to go to work. Work was a drag. Vivian and I were not seeing eye-to-eye, and I felt judged by my other co-workers. I was tired of being judged. I was tired of being manipulated for love. I was tired of being abused. I was tired of being labeled as a murderer. I was tired of feeling guilty for the rape, the molestation, the physical, mental, and verbal abuse. I was tired. So, I took my rest.

Emotional Murder
Volume 2

In *Emotional Murder, Volume 2*, readers are invited to continue the journey with Rhonda as she moves towards a path of healing. Be encouraged by her powerful testimony that comes as a result of overcoming deep pain and by rededicating her beliefs, principles and her life to God.

About the Author

Veronica Tucker has been a writer, director of drama ministry, licensed minister, evangelist, and field social worker.

Risen from an emotional grave and surviving generational affliction, Veronica denounced religion and adopted Kingdom. Veronica is a Kingdom citizen, ambassador, and daughter of the King of kings. Kingdom faith has set her free. Veronica has a remarkable gift for edifying and encouraging others driven by the passion to see others reach their full potential. She is known for empowering and equipping others. She worked with the Department of Disabilities and Special Needs where she remained for over twenty years. She is a first-generation college graduate. Her educational background includes a bachelor's and master's degree in social work. She loves to work with families, individuals, and couples in the community, providing individual and family counseling, crisis intervention, life skills, and conflicts resolution. She is also a spiritual life coach. Her goal is to continue empowering others by encouraging them not to allow their unfortunate circumstances to train wreck their futures. She pushes those around her, letting them know there are no limits.

FFKM is an organization established for the purpose of empowering and equipping Kingdom citizens to become the leaders of their generation, giving them the tools and resources to excel in every area of life utilizing Kingdom principles and Kingdom demonstrations. It also focuses on spirituality, education, and emotional development.

Resources

If you or someone you know are experiencing suicidal thoughts, or have been negatively triggered in any way, please seek spiritual or medical attention. For additional resources visit:

https://suicidepreventionlifeline.org/

https://www.noplace4hate.org/help-hotlines/

http://www.internationalhelpline.org/helpline

https://centers.rainn.org/

www.ingramcontent.com/pod-product-compliance
Lightning Source LLC
Chambersburg PA
CBHW020005290326
41935CB00007B/312